Brick walls and broken systems

One woman's way through
Maxine Griffiths' story

Annie Barrett

Gaynor Press

Published in 2026

All rights reserved. No part of this publication may be reproduced, stored in a retrieval system, or transmitted in any form or by any means, electronic, mechanical, photocopying, recording or otherwise, without prior permission of the publisher and copyright holders.

Copyright © Annie Barrett 2026

The moral rights of the author have been asserted.
anniebarrett.com.au

978-1-7642771-0-5 paperback

978-1-7642771-1-2 ebook

Gaynor Press

A catalogue record for this book is available from the National Library of Australia.

Cover design: Abdur Razzaque, Dhaka

Cover image: Maxine Griffiths, Hobart

Typeset in 12/17 Cochin

For Don

Contents

Part One
Childhood fragments: Parallel lives and seeking safety 1

Part Two
Creating homes: Risks, adventures and advocacy 73

Part Three
Generational healing: Happiness and loss 171

Epilogue 255

Acknowledgements 257

Author's note

Maxine Griffiths AM asked me to write her story. We are friends and were colleagues in disability and advocacy services in Tasmania. Maxine is a big picture person, memories, details, and documents are slightly blurred, resulting in some confusion around the accuracy of dates.

Some names in this story have been changed to protect privacy. I have used some language and terminology that was often used in the 1980s and 1990s that is recognised today as disempowering, discriminatory and inappropriate. Please accept my apologies for any offence.

Through my own research and interviews I have explored and given voice to Maxine's ideas and opinions throughout her story. For narrative purposes, some scenes have been imagined based upon Maxine's information and memories. Any errors in the story are mine.

Part One

Childhood fragments

Parallel lives and seeking safety

Chapter 1

Every child is precious. Especially this little one. Maxine nestled Don in her lap, nuzzled his soft brown hair and planted a kiss on his forehead. They sat in the garden of the Mothercraft home, a large two-storey timber building in Newtown, Hobart. As she cradled Don's awkward legs and floppy body Maxine made up stories and songs and showed him the patterns of light and shade through the leaves of the trees.

She believed he was intelligent, despite his labels: 'blind', 'spastic' and 'retarded'. She wanted to test him, so as they absorbed the warm sunshine, she sang him little songs.

'The birds in the trees …' and then slipped in the wrong words, nonsense like 'toast hanging in the trees …' Don looked up and then turned his head and looked at Maxine. He tried to reach out, but a spasm abruptly sent his arms flailing.

'Toast in the trees, see the toast in the trees,' she sang again. He laughed. She played simple finger games, chatted gently and giggled with him.

Maxine bathed, fed and played with the babies who were left at the home by their tired mothers. Even in the late 1970s doctors still recommended mothers leave their babies who struggled with sleeping or feeding problems at the Mothercraft home, to be settled into strict routines, allowing the Mums to rest back in their own homes.

Maxine's blue nurse's uniform with a white cap swam on her tiny frame. She looked like a child in a grown-up costume, a girl-woman even though she was nearly nineteen. She loved having three or four babies smelling gorgeous, lined up in bouncinettes. The nurses competed with each other as they warmed bottles and settled the twenty infants into Matron's strict schedules. After a few weeks the mothers visited Matron for instructions on her rigid craft of mothering, before taking their cherished ones home again.

Maxine's favourite little one was Don. He was different, a toddler nearly three years old, but he wasn't toddling. He couldn't walk or talk. He was always wobbling around and getting hurt and often had a large lump on his head, or a black eye.

Don was born in the Launceston General Hospital on 28th November 1973. He arrived early, feet first, a breech baby with the umbilical cord wrapped around his neck. His birth Mum had a long, painful labour and cried out for a caesarean. His skin had a bluish tinge and Don had to be revived. There was evidence that at some point he suffered a cerebral haemorrhage and brain damage.

It had been a difficult time for Don's biological parents before he was born, especially as Don's father had left his wife, late in her pregnancy. A few weeks after his birth Don was still in hospital. While his birth mother visited him, held him, and loved her vulnerable baby his prognosis was poor. The doctors thought he would probably never understand anything. In early December Don's birth mother initially signed consent for his adoption. However, because of his special needs he was taken into State Care.

The welfare approaches at the time were not often supportive of relinquishing parents. Mothers especially were told by the medical authorities, what was best for them and their babies often without explanations, choices, or compassionate care being offered. Some mothers were told to forget their babies and get on with their lives.

In February 1974, Don, was declared a ward of the State. During his first year between short stays with foster parents he was left lingering in hospital. In October 1974 he was transferred to the Mothercraft home in Hobart.

At mealtimes Maxine propped Don up in front of her on a pillow on her knees with a bench behind him and packed more pillows all around him.

'Look at the spoon, Don,' Maxine said and he did. 'Look at me, Don,' and he did. She tried to hold his back straight with one hand and feed him pureed food with the other. She wished the other nurses could see his intelligence. Maxine was the only one who thought he might not be 'retarded' or 'blind', just physically 'handicapped'.

Don slept in the sunroom to the right of the entrance where most of the babies were lined up in cots. His cot was in the corner of the draughty room. Each morning Maxine checked on Don, leaning over and stroking his face.

'We'll go out into the garden again later today.' She took his little hands in hers and tried to warm them. He was always cold.

At night Maxine listened to the babies: their cries and whimpers escaped the wards and floated upstairs where she lived with other nurses. She heard Don's plaintive cry. She lay still in her narrow bed and listened, wanting to go to him, but she was off duty and it was not her role to get up and feed or comfort him, like she had for her youngest brother, Tim. As the eldest of four, she had been looking after babies most of her life.

One wintery June day when Don was about three-and-a-half

years old, a white taxi pulled up outside the home. Maxine stood with the other nurses on the narrow steps, her face contained and her hands clenched. Matron had told her that this big day was coming. Maxine had packed Don's little brown box with a change of clothes: pants and a too-big, hand-knitted jumper. No socks, no shoes. A senior nurse carried Don to the taxi and laid him down on the back seat.

As the taxi drove off Maxine watched the white nurse's cap through the back window and hoped that Don was comfortable. *Does he even have a pillow to lie on?* She turned away and walked back up the steps. It was dark inside. She gathered up the sheets and blankets from Don's empty cot and held them to her chest, briefly smelling his sweet scent, before she took them to the laundry. She had to get on with her day, just as she'd had to when she was growing up. There were always jobs to do at home, clothes to fold and food to prepare, even in the midst of the grief or the horrible arguments of her childhood.

Along with the babies who were not thriving, there were a few other children like Don: a couple of children with spina bifida and another little girl with cerebral palsy. She was pretty with an infectious smile, and a favourite with the nurses. She was classed as more intelligent than Don.

'Why is she able to stay on here, when Don has to be sent away?' Maxine had asked matron a few days earlier.
'She has somewhere else to go when she is a little older, a small hostel,' Matron said.
'Can't Don go there too?' Maxine asked. 'No, no he is far too handicapped.'

~

The Mothercraft home was a dumping ground for children like Don while they waited their turn to go to the mental asylum, the Royal Derwent Hospital, the large institution up the Derwent River, at New Norfolk. Maxine thought the hospital was probably just a much larger dumping ground.

Don was sent up the river, but he had crept into her heart.

Chapter 2

Maxine had left school at the end of Year 10 and trained to be a mothercraft nurse. It seemed a good fit and the best thing was, it came with live-in accommodation. In Tasmania, High School finished at Year 10 and then, for Years 11 and 12, students went onto Matriculation College. Young people who lived in the Huon Valley or other rural areas had to get up to Hobart to finish school, which came with many extra costs.

Maxine had started school late and missed chunks, weeks, months with house moves and looking after her brothers and sister. She had heard it was easier to stay on at school on the mainland. Most of her classmates finished school at Year 10 and immediately got married! She could have done that; there was a boy, a keen boy.

Her grandmother had given her a sharp warning. 'Don't you ever go off and have children too young now.' *Not going to let that happen, no way.*

She was not going to fall pregnant and be trapped like her Mum. Her parents, Colleen and Maxwell had made a fine young couple, as they rode around on Maxwell's motorbike, with Colleen's thick dark hair and olive skin and Maxwell, not tall but handsome, with short dark hair. But then Colleen was just sixteen and didn't know how the baby inside was going to come out. They were still kids themselves when they got married.

They lived in Pelverata in a two-room hut when Maxine was a baby. There she crawled and explored and climbed into the sooty cold fireplace and was smudged with grime. Colleen found seasonal work when she could on the hut owner's farm, picking small fruit to earn enough money for food, leaving baby Maxine with a neighbour.

Maxine's family had lived a bit like nomads mostly in the south but occasionally up north. Her Dad found work where he could, moving about from one farm to the next, and a sawmill here and there. They struggled through winters where the sun slipped down early behind the hills and the mountain, leaving a cold damp in the valleys around the Huon River, south of Hobart. Inside the old farmhouses there were never enough beds, with extended family often visiting. But somehow there was always enough food, Maxwell shot rabbits, and the family fished and foraged for mushrooms and berries.

Her brother, Geoff, arrived when Maxine was four years old and, soon after, her sister Sherry came along. Maxine proudly helped her mother around the house and with the little ones. When Geoff was old enough, he went out into the paddocks on the weekends with Maxine and their Dad. Both children helped in the veggie garden and gathered up the warm eggs from the chook shed. Geoff was chubby with brown hair, charming with his bright eyes and olive skin just like his Mum's, and often up to mischief. As the eldest, it was Maxine's job to watch out for him. Somebody had to. On warm evenings she, Geoff and Sherry snuggled in their Dad's arms in the backyard before tea. Maxine knew Geoff was her Mum's favourite. Colleen held him close.

Another baby arrived unexpectedly when Maxine was thirteen, a gorgeous little soft bundle, held proudly by her Dad. They called him Tim, the miracle baby. When Tim cried in the night, Maxine, bleary-eyed, fumbled out of bed to feed him before her parents woke. It wasn't an expectation but she warmed a bottle, and settled him. He gurgled and she stroked his soft hair, nestled in and smelt his innocent baby scent.

After Tim was born Maxine's Mum didn't seem to have strength anymore for doing anything around the house.

'Mum's having a rest,' her Dad told her. 'She is being looked after. We just have to make do at home together.'

There were adult whisperings. Maxine heard someone say a 'breakdown'. Her Mum had a few stints in hospital and at the Peacock Rest Home. During one of those times, a family friend was looking after baby Tim, and Maxine and Sherry went with their Dad to visit him.

'Let's bring Tim home, Dad,' Maxine said. 'I'll stay home from school and look after him.'

'Do you think you could manage?' her Dad asked.

'Of course, I look after him mostly, anyway.' So, for a few weeks her Dad gave her shopping money. Maxine enjoyed bossing her little sister, Sherry, and singing and cooing to her baby brother while she fed, changed him and settled him to sleep in the old family pram.

~

Maxine was restless at the Mothercraft home after Don was sent away and not long afterwards, before completing her training, she left. She was reluctantly back at home on the weekends and back at school too, having a go at matriculation at the college up in Hobart. *It is a messy time; yes, that's the word, messy,* she thought as the Monday morning bus threaded its way towards Hobart. School was interesting but difficult. She didn't see how she could make it all work.

Maxine's ride into college gave her time to gaze out the bus window as the early light revealed fields of hops and dairy farms.

Back home in Huonville her Dad would be rugged up and striding out in the paddocks, hands behind his back, full of purpose. Her brother and sister would be getting ready for school.

The bus climbed the slow winding roads and Maxine looked at the familiar weatherboard cottages in Fern Tree on the slopes of the mountain, beside the tall gums, ferns and rocky waterfalls. It was too far to return to Huonville each day and the buses were infrequent. As more than an hour dragged on, she wondered where she could stay that week, maybe her friend's couch? Maxine couldn't go to her other friend, with a mattress on the floor. That was last week. And how was she going to keep paying for the bus? Her parents couldn't afford it.

~

The image of Don's little body cradled in her arms often slipped into her mind especially when she looked after other children in a new childcare centre. Her training in the Mothercraft home had helped her find the job a few months after she had finally given up school and left home again.

During the heady days of Gough Whitlam's Labor Government, the first funded-childcare training was developed at Hobart Technical College. It was free; there was course work, childcare placements and financial support. Maxine enrolled, hoping it could be her lucky break; she wanted to work with children like Don.

In her dreams there were glimpses of Don, a smile, then it was gone. Shivering one morning in the poky bedsit she managed to rent in Hobart, she remembered warming his little hands. *Had anyone else done that for him?* She felt scared for him. The stories up at the institution at New Norfolk were of ghastly 'mad' people, not fragile little children. *Was he even still alive?*

Maxine was worried she had deserted Don, even though she had only known him for a short while at the Mothercraft home. She wanted to see him but didn't know how to. She couldn't rock up to that huge hospital at New Norfolk to visit him. She was a young country girl in the city. She wasn't family, she was nobody special.

Chapter 3

At the end of July 1978, Maxine and another student drove beside the Derwent River. Mt Wellington, now called Kunanyi/Mt Wellington, was starkly outlined in deep grey-browns and tinged by purple. The changes on the mountain touched people's moods with clear sunny days, wisps and swirls of cloud, lashing winds and snow. They left its towering presence behind and went past housing estates, flanked by hills on the left and the river on the right. They saw the smoking stacks of the paper mill and drove on through the main street of New Norfolk to the Royal Derwent Hospital, Australia's oldest mental asylum. Maxine had managed to arrange a placement there during her childcare training.

'Why on earth would you want to go up there?' another student had asked Maxine. 'That place is for "retards"!'

Like everyone else, Maxine had heard the stories about the hospital; anyone who was different was sent there. Isolated at New Norfolk, the patients were out of sight and out of mind. It was a one-way street. If you were sent up the river you never came back.

Maxine had first met children with disabilities when she was in high school. Those lunchtimes when she went out with a small group of teenage girls for social service were one of the best things about her schooldays. The girls walked up the narrow winding country road to Huonville Special School, a large sprawling house near the Huon River. Maxine chose to feed the children with the most severe disabilities. She chatted, giggled with them as she pulled faces and made up silly rhymes and waited for the right moment, when the child's mouth was both open and hopefully a little relaxed and in went a spoonful of soft warm lunch. She was good at it.

Not many at her high school wanted to mess with mashed food that slipped off the spoon or was spat out, or change the nappies of older children on the bench in the open bathroom. But already in high school Maxine had a sense of the injustices such children faced, as well as their vulnerability.

At home she had become vigilant and she carried that awareness with her everywhere. She had learned to listen and watch for changes in the adults' voices and moods, to notice who was in the house, and which relatives were the safest to be around.

Even as a young child she monitored herself and the situation, gauging if it was better to stay outside and play or go inside and look after the younger ones?

Maxine and her friend drove though the Royal Derwent gates, down the tree-lined avenue and into the extensive grounds of the hospital adjacent to the town. It stretched across hills down a creek bed and up the other side.

The wail of a child reverberated across the courtyard. Maxine gulped in a breath of fresh air and turned to take in her surroundings. Figures rambled in the distance. With a tingling of excitement and some trepidation, she was keen to meet the children and hoped she could find Don.

The institution was imposing; in all directions were red-brick colonial Georgian buildings, and great long separated wards. Across the creek bed was the large commercial laundry where some of the 'inmates' worked, washing the hospital clothes. Hundreds of people lived in the hospital; some lived their whole lives there, many locked in.

In the afternoon Maxine found her way to M ward, the children's ward. As she entered, she was assaulted by the heat and the reeking odour of urine, stale cabbage and overcooked food. She glanced around the bare walls and, on mattresses on the floor lay children scarcely clothed. There were no warm greetings, no introductions and no clear expectations of what her duties were.

'This boy needs toileting,' a nurse said later, 'and you'll help feed the children.' *Easy*, Maxine thought.

When they gathered for a break, the staff smoked, talked about their days off but ignored Maxine. She felt like an outsider; like they didn't want her there. She headed down a wide corridor; a lingering smell of disinfectant clung to the dull walls. She hoped she had the right ward.

Then she saw Don, lying on the floor on a dingy mattress and she hurried across the room to his side. But, not wanting to jolt him, she slowed. By now she felt eager and hot.

He didn't seem to have grown much since she had seen him at the Mothercraft home. He was still skinny, pale and tiny. His head looked too big and his eyes bulged as though he was dehydrated. One leg was bent and she noticed again, as a spasm jerked his body, that he had no control over his movements.

'Do you remember me, Don?' Maxine stroked his short lank pale brown hair. His eyes flickered and there was a slight movement across his face. A hint of a smile?

'Over here,' a nurse called from down the corridor. Don

cringed. Maxine stood up. She looked at the figure walking away in her blue uniform with a cigarette dangling from her fingers. Maxine turned back to Don, longing for a spark of recognition.

'I'm so happy to see you again, I'll come back and find you later.'

Maxine was given tasks with other children, the less disabled, more mobile children, never Don. It was best to keep quiet, not talk about him; she did as she was told, she knew how to do that.

She soundlessly walked the grey hospital corridors. She had learned as a child to diligently do her jobs around the house and to slip out of rooms to avoid the fighting. She had kept watch, kept quiet, and looked after her sister and brothers.

One day, as instructed, she took a little boy and sat him on the toilet for his toilet training session. He started to cry loudly. The nurse came into the bathroom, where there were lines of toilets with no doors, picked up the boy and gave his bare bottom a hard smack. She then plopped him back on the toilet seat. Maxine flinched. She looked up at the woman but the nurse had already turned away. Nothing was said to the boy or to Maxine but she dressed the child, treating him gently, getting awkward legs into pants. Then, she took him, still whimpering, into the room for his meal.

'If you don't stop crying you won't get no tea,' another nurse told the boy. Maxine sat beside him, talking softly, trying to spoon some mashed slops into his mouth, hoping he might calm down and eat some food, but he kept crying. His food was taken away.

Another day at mealtime a child had a mishap and spilt his food. He was scolded by a staff member for being naughty, then grabbed under his armpits and dropped onto the floor and sworn at. He cried. His food was taken away too. Maxine glanced around; her shoulders tensed. No one took any notice. *Why didn't they care more? Why didn't anyone say anything?*

~

Maxine saw things she could not unsee. Some of the children were shut all day in the day room, with bare walls and a few tables and chairs. They rocked back and forth on the linoleum floor. They climbed over one another and urinated wherever they happened to be, on window ledges, on the floor. Some were left in soiled nappies. There were puddles of urine, sometimes vomit too, while the staff, both men and women, chatted in the glassed-in nurses' station in the centre of the ward and smoked and watched television, their backs to the children.

One day Maxine simply went and found a mop and cleaned up the smelly mess that had been ignored by the staff.

Had all these children been abandoned like Don? Maxine didn't have much time to spare, but when she did, she sought out Don. She plonked herself on the ground, chatted with him and they played with some damaged toys she'd managed to find. When he smiled it felt like a warm embrace across her chest. She also watched Don from a distance and saw him physically recoil from other people.

When Maxine helped out with feeding the children she chatted away or sang a song and watched their mouths and throats, waited for their jaws to soften, then spooned in some food. She saw Don at mealtimes and noticed he was often fed lying down.

She wanted to say to the staff, *You try swallowing on your back.* But she didn't. She knew by then it was best to keep quiet.

The staff rarely spoke to Maxine or, for that matter, to the children. She was an intruder, a smart aleck from college. Maxine didn't even know their names. They were cold and wore no identification. The female workers were dominating, ferocious, like a gang that you wouldn't dare cross.

Maxine didn't know how to make an official complaint, but she had to say something. She had yet to develop her steely uncompromising activism, but she could not remain silent. Halfway through her student placement, Maxine went into the office of a senior staff member and told him what she had seen. Two days later she was interviewed by three senior men and repeated the allegations. She then left the hospital, extremely distressed.

Her placement was cut short.

Chapter 4

Maxine only witnessed a snapshot of M ward life at Royal Derwent Hospital during her six days there. But its bleakness felt familiar, a barren feeling like she had as a child. At Royal Derwent children like Don with severe physical disabilities were called 'imbeciles'. Although Don and other children were not 'mentally insane' they lived in the mental institution. Doctors also referred to Don as an 'unfortunate' child, with athetoid cerebral palsy quadriplegia. He had involuntary movements, spasms in his thin arms and weak legs, and was assumed to be blind with severe mental retardation.

~

The whispers of change were flowing in the late 1970s and the sweeping progress brought in by the Whitlam Labor government slowly filtered down to Tasmania. Women explored their rights and individual choices and members of the Aboriginal communities were demanding recognition of identity, culture and land rights. Environmentalists lost their fight to save Lake Pedder in 1972 but the Tasmanian Wilderness Society was established in 1976 and they were gearing up for another battle to save the Franklin River. Yet children with disabilities, whose rights were yet to be acknowledged, were still abandoned and hidden away.

Don and the other children on M ward lived in a part of the hospital known as Willow Court, named after a massive willow tree planted in the early days of the colony by Lady Jane Franklin. The original Willow Court Barracks had housed convict invalids, road gangs, and the insane. That was the male legacy infused into the institution. Confusingly, over the years the terms Royal Derwent and Willow Court were used interchangeably.

Royal Derwent Hospital was the factory for New Norfolk, the prime employer apart from hops in the old agricultural days. Staff were mostly untrained. They chose to work long 12-hour shifts, two days on, two days off. Patients' symptoms were not well managed medically so there were physical restraints; children were strapped into their cots with bandages. They looked out with vacant expressions, often unkempt and dirty, some with matted hair. It was a scary place for families and their visits were merely tolerated. Their children were classed as uneducable and many families had been told to leave their children in the care of the State and to forget about them.

Despite there being things the staff might have done to support the children's play, create stimulating activities, care and comfort, they simply, fed and medicated them. They lived for their two days off. There were a few good people who genuinely cared, but the entrenched systems didn't support them. And the senior authorities were cut off from the reality of the people in their care. Some staff became victims too. Workers developed mental health problems and became 'inmates' themselves, their whole grim lives swallowed up by the hospital.

The food was all mass-produced, overcooked mush. Some of

the children, including Don, had feeding difficulties, trouble with swallowing and chewing; they often had strong tongue thrusts and poor head control. Feeding them simply took a long time. If the staff couldn't be bothered to persevere, then children didn't get fed properly.

In some wards, the hygiene was less than adequate; there was only one toothbrush, for example, for a group of children.

Workers carried around huge heavy keys to enter the locked wards. The atmosphere in the teenage ward was terrifying; these young people were, in effect imprisoned, yet were strong and mobile. There was nothing for them to do except wander around their dayroom, no education, no activities. But the teenagers were experiencing raging hormones, there was masturbation and violence. Sexual abuse stories abounded. There were rumoured pregnancies and abortions.

In H ward, where some of the older people lived, dinnertime was at 4.30 pm. They often ate without cutlery, shovelling their food in with their fingers. Some of them sat naked as they had soiled or wet themselves earlier.

Clothes went to the huge industrial onsite laundry where some of the patients worked; the care for the clothing wasn't as good as it might be and shirts and trousers often got chewed up and spat out. Staff may have looked for clean clothes at the end of the day, but sometimes there was nothing left, not even any of the institutional green pyjamas, until the laundry came the next day. H ward was a locked ward. Nobody from outside went in there.

In one storeroom near the ward there were thick cardboard boxes and old leather suitcases that patients had brought with them forty or fifty years previously. All that was personal had long gone; the luggage remained empty and stored on ledges.

This is what lay ahead for Don when he became older – his poor physical condition, recurrent infections, and a vulnerability to pneumonia would be ongoing problems. Would he and the other children on M ward even survive?

Chapter 5

When Maxine was in her late teens and early twenties there wasn't much choice of nightlife in Hobart apart from the new Casino. Alone, she often slipped inside its tall brash façade and into the series of cave-like bars with dimmed artificial lights, endless drinking and nooks for couples and those on the make. This was a sacred money palace.

When she perched her scrawny frame on a stool, with a near empty glass of whiskey in her hand, her childcare studies and part-time job of looking after little children were quickly forgotten. She watched the men in their suits and jackets and the women in high heels as they played the tables and wondered about her high-school crushes on girls. She wanted adult connection and conversation but did not want anyone to come too close. She befriended lonely men, safe with anonymity.

She sipped her whiskey and remembered all the fuss about the Casino. Tasmania, the island often left off the map of Australia, had claimed another first. Despite opposition, Wrest Point Casino in Hobart was the first casino built on Australian shores. Her parents had not wanted all those greedy mainlanders coming to Hobart; they thought Tassie was fine as it was.

The Casino jutted out on a sunny point in Sandy Bay,

overlooking the Derwent River, but that location had a dark past. In the early days of the colony, it was a place for hangings.

The Casino was a long way down river from Don at New Norfolk where nearly 150 years earlier, in 1827, the Royal Derwent Hospital, the first mental asylum in Australia, was established.

Pip's wine bar in the city was another well patronised local haunt. The large barn-like room, was smoky but airy at the same time. Hobart was still a small capital city where locals vaguely knew each other. Maxine was a familiar sight as she strode the streets, generally alone.

One night, Maxine was at the bar, it was late and still warm in March 1978. She looked up and saw a tall solid man, talking to the guitarist. He walked over to the bar.

'He's good, isn't he?' he indicated over his shoulder.

'Yeah, they're great,' she smiled. 'I like it here.'

'I'm Paul,' he said. 'I've seen you here before and around Hobart.'

'Yes, hi, Maxine.' She didn't tell him that she had a crush on that guitarist.

It was a full night in the bar, nearly 200 people were in the room. The blues and roots and covers were working.

Paul and Maxine leant into each other at the bar while around them the crowd sang along with 'Mercedes Benz'.

They wandered onto the dance floor and moved separately, together, and smiled, while the throng swirled around them. Between sets they talked some more.

Paul told her about growing up on the family farm at Sorell, north of Hobart. He spoke slowly and quietly; he seemed thoughtful. She liked that.

It could have been a fleeting meeting. Maxine had met others in this way on the nights she went alone and late to bars and to the Casino.

But that evening was the beginning of a friendship that would prove both enduring and ambiguous. After that first night they met at Pip's quite often and after midnight, they went to Mummy's in Battery Point, an all-night café. There, Maxine had her only meal of the day, melted cheese on toast.

At about two am they went their separate ways into the cold Tasmanian night.

'Have you ever been up to Willow Court?' Maxine asked Paul one night later that year over a drink at the Traveller's Rest. She had been thinking about Don more and more, and unusually for her, needed to talk.

'I've heard lots, but no I haven't,' said Paul. 'Why?'

She told Paul about Don, stuck in the awful children's ward.

'I am really worried about him. I feel this strange connection with him; he just touched my heart; it was there immediately when I first met him at the Mothercraft home. It's so strong, I can't let it go.'

'Can people visit up there?' Paul asked.

'Yeah, but it is complicated,' Maxine said. 'The staff don't like outsiders going in, especially me. They hate me up there, I complained. But I might try and see him soon.'

Around Hobart many people assumed Maxine and Paul were lovers. *It was silly the way people gossiped. It was nobody's business.* Paul was clever with words, she liked that, and he was observant, read the papers and met people from different walks of life. There was always something interesting to talk about. But he was getting too close. Occasionally he looked at her in 'that way', like some other men did. That was a problem, confusing. He was not pushy; it was just like he was trying to be romantic but he didn't know how. Maxine wasn't going to let anyone get clingy. It made her skin crawl, like invisible ants climbing up her arm.

She tried to like him more, maybe even tried to love him, but it didn't work. It was awkward and Paul was tentative.

'You don't eat much, Maxine,' Paul said one night. He bought some chips at the bar along with their whiskies. 'Don't you get hungry?'

'No, well yes, I eat when I'm hungry, but not like three meals a day.' She liked feeling thin, sort of empty inside, no feeling. Yet there were veiled childhood feelings and memories.

When she was little, about six, she stopped talking; just kept quiet, except for 'please' and 'thank you'. She hoped her parents might have stopped yelling and throwing things, but they didn't notice her silence or her small, frail body always shaking with dread. Innocent and vulnerable, no one spoke for her.

'You are a good, quiet little girl aren't you?' Visitors had reinforced her mute self. She had sat at the table with adults, invisible as she observed and listened to all kinds of talk. But she did get to eat lots of chocolate, her reward for being so quiet, so good.

As a child, she could make herself unheard and unseen but this was different. As an adult she could do whatever she liked. She could choose to eat, or not. She was tall but she could make herself invisible and make herself noticed like at the Casino. It felt powerful. She was in control.

Chapter 6

When she was sixteen years old – the same age her Mum had given birth to her – Maxine's usual practice would be to come home from school, go straight into her room and close the door.

'Is she alright?' her Dad asked while he scrubbed his hands in the laundry.

'Writing poetry, I think,' her Mum said, from the kitchen where she was scrubbing potatoes.

'Oh, I thought she was doing her homework,' her Dad said.

Maxine listened behind the closed door. She smiled. She didn't really care what they thought. She lay on her bed reading. There were very few books at home but Maxine had discovered the local library and thrilling other worlds beckoned, worlds of exploring freedom like Somerset Maugham's *Of Human Bondage*.

She had discovered the delights of classical records too. But really, she just wanted to leave home. Not sure where she would fit in life, she was going to get out and do something and be somebody one day.

She didn't want to think about the stuff that went on at home but memories slipped in as she escaped into her books and music. When she was about nine years old, she had loved watching the clouds, lying on the grass in the paddock outside, even if it was spiky on her legs. When it rained, she heard the Huon River at the end of the paddocks, as it raced past. She didn't care if she got soaking wet, it was only water, but it made her Mum cross. Her Dad didn't seem to mind. He didn't seem to mind much about anything except her Mum's shouting and things hurled around.

One night there was a thud and a clatter as something hit the wall; a cup maybe and Maxine couldn't slip past them through the kitchen, out the back door, down the three steps, across the back yard and into the paddock to escape. Her Mum had been stewing the rabbit they shot yesterday; there was a meaty, potato and gravy smell coming from the kitchen as well as horrible words. She blocked out the words, she could do that, just go somewhere else in herself. Her uncles had taught her that, even though they didn't know it. She wished she could run away. *But who would look after her brother and sister?*

It had gone quiet, but she didn't dare go out yet. She moved her pillow around and lay back down with her hands behind her back. She rolled over and lay on her tummy, she felt tummy-ache bad and sick. She shoved her face into the pillow and tried holding her breath but that didn't stop the discomfort. She gasped, but didn't like the sound she heard, a sort of sobbing. *Why do people have to hurt other people? It wasn't fair; poor Dad.*

'Be a good girl, Maxine, for your mother.' Her Dad's words rolled around in her head. He always said that when he had to go to work and didn't take her with him. She wanted to be good for him. She liked her Dad more than her Mum. *Was that allowed?* It was best with him, doing things outside, busy, beside him on the tractor, and staying well behind him when he went rabbiting. She didn't like the shotgun but she liked rabbit stew.

~

Maxine knew her Mum, Colleen, had had a hard childhood. And that her parents were maybe trapped within their young marriage.

Colleen slipped into rages as quickly as she forgot them. She did not seem to be herself. She was not well, and was unable to manage stress, a husband, children and poverty and still carry some responsibility for her younger brothers as well. Yet, later, Maxine recognised that Colleen did her best.

Maxine stored away snippets of family stories that she had overheard, of her Mum's poor family in the backblocks of Tasmania, near Oatlands, with her four brothers. Housing was cheaper there and there was work in the mill for her father.

Before her family lived in Oatlands Colleen had run freely around North Hobart and the city when she was a young girl.

The family shared a home with her mother Pearl's parents, in Harrington Street. When she was about five, Colleen and one of her brothers ran into a nearby police station and pretended they were lost. Inside, they were fed and given milk or lemonade and soon after, they quickly escaped and ran home. Colleen really wanted to attend school and so she walked from Harrington Street up to the Goulburn St Primary School and asked if she could join the classes even though she wasn't old enough to go to school.

Later, when Colleen had to leave school early to look after the household and find a job; she worked in the biscuit factory and, later, a peg factory.

Maxine wondered if there was shouting and hitting in her Mum's family, back then too?

During occasional night-time arguments between her parents,

Maxine needed to block out the sounds as she drifted off to sleep, but fibro walls didn't cushion much. One incident, when Maxine was older involved her seeing her Mum waving a gun around. Living on farms there were always rifles around, but that night Colleen pointed it at her Dad, Maxwell. He was trying to calm Colleen.

'Put it down.' Maxine heard her Dad say and she raced into the kitchen and saw them.

'Stop!' Maxine shouted and stepped in between them.

The gun went off. It just missed Maxwell's ear. Colleen dropped the gun and grabbed a sauce bottle from the kitchen table and threw it at Maxine, screaming at her to get out. Maxwell walked away, said nothing.

Chapter 7

Maxine surprised herself when she talked with Paul. Normally she kept private compartments within herself for her different friends, friends she often met through her various jobs or studies; some became her lovers. It was like she lived separate lives. Her feelings were tucked away, hidden.

But over months and then years, her friendship with Paul deepened and she told him stuff, sometimes even muddled emotions, more about Don and bits about her family, but they mostly talked about ideas. She loved that, bouncing thoughts around, the conservation debate that was taking off in Hobart, and ethics, principles, philosophy. Over time she told Paul about her lovers, both men and women, but not everything.

One evening Maxine and Paul were back at Pip's wine bar. Maxine had been going out with Kay for a while, but it had become difficult. Kay was small, stocky, and needy. She wore jeans and a t-shirt and her hair was cropped short. She wrote Maxine endless love poems.

'Kay has just walked in,' Paul said, indicating someone behind Maxine.

'Really? Again? She just keeps turning up,' Maxine said. 'I've got to go. She is doing weird stuff I don't like.' Maxine gulped down her wine pushed her chair back and left while Kay had her back to them. She had felt too ashamed to tell Paul what was happening; that her girlfriend was stalking her and had become violent.

~

There was more, a lot more that she hadn't told anyone. Like about the nights when she was little and she had felt smothered, crushed in her single bed that she sometimes had to share with one of her teenage uncles and their fumbling hands and pressing bodies. She had clung to the edge of her mattress. She had already learnt, by the age of six, that if you told, people got upset and then there was more trouble. Or nothing changed. Like when she told her Dad about her step grandfather.

'Daddy, Poppy is touching me,' little Maxine said one day.

She thought that Daddies were meant to be brave.

When she woke early in the morning Maxine wrapped her slippers around her blue toes, and ran past Poppy's door, down the steps across the slippery wet path to the outside loo. Bang, she locked the door, gulped in some air, her heart pounding. Then, ran back past his room to her bed, hoping he didn't see her, hoping he wasn't awake to come and find her.

'Well stay away from him,' her Dad said.

'I do stay away but he still finds me,' Maxine said. 'Well stay away further, then.'

It was no different when she was an adult, a young adult, twenty years old. There was a man who must have followed her home from somewhere, the pub, maybe the Casino. He had looked vaguely familiar. *Had he been watching her just that night or for a while?* He raped her in the small bedsit she rented in Campbell Street.

She went to the police but they didn't seem interested. It was before the times when kind women doctors did a forensic examination following a rape allegation. Young women were questioned about their clothes and behaviour. Short skirts, out alone, asking for it?

After that horrible suffocating night, the rapist seemed to be everywhere still watching, still following. She had to find somewhere else to live. She moved into a condemned house across the river in Brighton, it was dark and a shambles, but it was safe.

Maxine had already learned to shove her experiences and feelings into separate boxes and close them off, away somewhere, her Poppy, her uncles. *No, no more thoughts. Away. Done.*

Chapter 8

Maxine erected her flimsy two-person tent, unpacked her large orange pack and sat on the ground in a caravan park in Devonport. Her skeletal undernourished frame was draped in shorts and a man's shirt. Her hair was cut boy-like. With a cup of whiskey in hand, she looked across to a man, thirtyish. She had arrived from a hitchhiking trip from Hobart as she often did during the summer between jobs and studies.

It was mainly truckies who gave her much appreciated lifts in their huge rigs. Some scolded her for taking risks on the road, a young woman, alone, thumb out as if the world never cared less. Or she didn't care less. What those truckies didn't know was just how much risk there had been in her childhood back in the Huon Valley.

A life on the road seemed a better place to be. She thought she could have done with some caring truckies back then as she tumbled through her childhood.

As she thumbed her way around Tassie she often met up with fellow campers, especially men – not from her want – but she was female, young and alone. She had street wisdom, like a stealthy leopard, watching, ready. She learned that the scruffier and more bedraggled men offered more safety than others. This man in the

Devonport campground, sitting across from her had long hair, rough clothes and an open face.

They shared drinks, and conversation. She was relaxed and curious. Perhaps it was the alcohol that allowed her to calm down, breathe deeply into herself, relieved at not needing to look behind her, with flight mode at the ready.

Later, his stare stayed with her and she remembered deep penetrating eyes that rested on her face and occasionally there was a smile.

'Who do you want to become?' He asked questions about who she was. 'What are your dreams and aspirations?'

Many hours passed.

'Well cheerio,' Maxine finally said standing up. It was time to end the night.

'I would like to meet you again in about thirty years' time,' the man said, 'to see and hear about you. I think you have deep wisdom which will play out in remarkable ways.'

Back in her thinly lined sleeping bag she wondered what he meant. Rolling over, she made a mental note to file away his words.

The next morning, as the sun rose to yet another beautiful summer morning she awoke to birds, the squeals of small children and waves pounding the beach nearby. Firing up her kerosene stove to make tea she wandered over to the man's campsite. But no, nothing, no evidence of him. She wondered if she had dreamt him, their conversation, his words, and his deep listening.

~

Maxine finished her childcare training in 1979. After her curtailed six days at Willow Court another placement was organised for her at a childcare centre. But there were times she arrived late or didn't show up at all, or phone in either. She was coping, just, with those hidden away life fragments. Her childcare course supervisor thought she was unreliable. Maxine struggled to complete the course, but despite her tardiness, she always received glowing reports for her work; all recognising that she related beautifully with the children in her care.

During her training she saw an advertisement asking for information about the treatment or neglect of patients at Royal Derwent Hospital, including Willow Court. She provided a statement and, later, was called as a witness at the *1979 Royal Derwent Hospital and Millbrook Rise Hospital Board of Inquiry.*

It was a year after her childcare placement there. The officials sat around a table, their setting felt formal. She felt small and alone, like a criminal under interrogation and was younger than everyone else. She described in detail what she had seen during her student placement at Willow Court, but it became her word against that of the staff. She was cross-examined, was accused of being a disaffected unreliable witness and of lying. Who was telling the truth?

She tried to explain how she learnt to work with so-called 'normal' children and that it should not make any difference that a child lived with a disability.

'You can still play with them and tell them stories.'

The Inquiry also heard from parents who visited their children at the institution and found they had infected wounds, unexplained bruises or bite marks, some children cowered as though about to be hit. Some saw flies crawling all over a sedated child. Another child had scabies.

One girl needed to wear a helmet for self-protection from

constant falls, but she often took it off and hid it. She had repeated head wounds and, when her parents visited, her hair was matted and her scalp infected; she was barely conscious. They took her to hospital.

Endless horror stories of neglect and abuse were recorded in the Inquiry. Reports said the children were smelly, dirty and naked, and overmedicated. The lack of staff training was a problem and was recognised in the report. There was also a reference to inadequate investigations of patient deaths.

Maxine's evidence was finally vindicated.

> "The physical abuse of child inmates of 'M' Ward did occur substantially in the manner claimed by the informant Miss Griffiths. The degree of violence was not such as to have other than a superficial effect and no injury, other than emotional trauma, was suffered."

And Don? He was stuck up there in M ward with no one to look out for him. *Was he still okay? Surviving, just?*

Chapter 9

Maxine dived into professional childcare work and her series of 'firsts' began. She became the first ever play leader on the children's ward at the Royal Hobart Hospital in the city. She loved working with the seriously-ill children, creating games and stories, playing with them on their sterile ward, making a mess with paper, crayons, paints and toys.

The following year – Maxine was still only twenty-three when she was asked to take on the coordination of the childcare centre at Bridgewater, a tough Housing Commission area. This isolated area with no public transport, shops or services, had many young families and single mums living there. It was the first community-based childcare centre in Tasmania and she supervised two staff.

Looking after the little children, cooking, painting and reading stories, wasn't even work, really. And it was such a relief to earn money. She never wanted to rely on anyone and certainly didn't want anyone dependent on her. People let you down. With her own money no one could tell her what to do. And now she was her own boss.

Maxine gave herself a new look: dyed her hair purple, and later bleached it white.

Her mind brimmed with ideas for the centre and she consulted and included the parents; her first project was to set up a toy library.

'But the kids and the families will steal them.'

'So, they must need them,' Maxine said.

The children were so different from the vulnerable children at Willow Court. At Bridgewater Maxine had two-year-olds telling her to 'fuck off'. One child escaped and ran home.

'Oh, that doesn't matter, he knows how to get in,' his parent said when she phoned.

Maxine was confident, a quick learner, and flexible; she discovered community development on the run. And she thought of little Don, voiceless, except for cries, and trapped in his body wherever he was left. It had been more than a year since she had seen him.

Maxine knew intuitively that children with disabilities should mix with children without disabilities. This was unheard of in the general community and ideas about care, but to her it was common sense. Willow Court was across the Derwent River, not far from Bridgewater, so, to have a trial integration scheme, she lobbied for a few children with disabilities to come down to her centre. She had to convince her committee, but they were happy enough; she worked hard and ran a good show and it would benefit the other children in the centre. The Commonwealth Government funded the childcare centre and she managed to negotiate additional funding.

Willow Court was harder to convince. She approached Alison Jacob, a new young teacher and psychologist employed to develop education programs for the children with severe disabilities.

Maxine had already met Alison during her childcare training.

She had been relieved to meet her, an authentic, energetic person with similar values who believed in giving time to children with the most severe disabilities.

Alison didn't appear to fear the system. She was one of a new breed of energetic professionals, keen for change. She brought fresh eyes to the wards; they soon became horrified eyes. Maxine didn't know it then, but Alison was to become an invaluable ally.

~

There had been a school on site at the hospital since 1959 but only for the higher functioning children and young people, those who could be trained to perform light industrial tasks. Alison worked with the children with more severe disabilities.

'What are you doing?' staff said to her when she started work at Willow Court. 'You'll never teach them anything.'

But Alison broke down simple tasks of self-care and living skills, encouraging small steps into learning. And she slowly worked towards institutional change.

Alison had been to many similar institutions on the mainland, but M ward, where Don lived, was the worst. One day Alison was teaching and in the morning a boy from her class went to the on-site dentist.

The day wore on and he didn't come back to school after lunch. She asked one of the staff where he was.

'Oh,' the worker said, 'he died under anaesthetic.'

~

After Maxine had given evidence at the Inquiry, she believed that the staff at Willow Court despised her. The same people were still there – once employed they never left. But she still needed to negotiate with the authorities, if her idea of integrating children with disabilities into her childcare centre was going to work. And she wanted Don to be included.

'You cannot deny these children this opportunity! Why would you?' she said to senior staff at Willow Court. 'It's a simple outing to play with other children. They shouldn't be locked away all the time.'

Maxine stepped into the first of many complex negotiations. Fortunately, Alison Jacob, who soon became the School Principal at Willow Court, understood her idea was good.

Maxine stood at the sink washing out paint brushes when the taxi finally arrived with the children from Willow Court. She was thrilled and longed to see Don again. He wasn't at school yet but with Alison's help Maxine had managed to include him in the project. Because he was a Ward of the State, Maxine and Alison had needed to secure approval from Royal Derwent Hospital, but also the State Welfare Department, his legal guardian. And medical approval had to be given. Maxine hoped he was well enough on the day to come.

She dried her hands and went to greet them. And Don was passed to her. He was a tiny, pale thing, lethargic, with his hair knotted and sticking out like a rag doll. Her heart raced as Don nestled into her arms. Maxine was dying to give him experiences of water play, of painting, of noisy kids, of lying in the sandpit. Later that day she prepared a big tub of water.

'Let's all wash the dollies,' Maxine said. The children helped Don stretch his hands into the warm soapy water and Maxine stroked his arm and folded his stiff fingers around a doll.

Maxine wanted more for Don, more of the good stuff of

her own childhood, being in nature, the fresh air, the farms. Don kept coming to her childcare centre, and she started visiting him at Willow Court. She sought approval to take him out on weekends.

Chapter 10

One warm Saturday she drove to new Norfolk, stepped out of her orange Mini Minor, crossed the car park, entered M ward and faced the same stale odours, the same staff. She could hear Don before she saw him, his familiar cries and groans. He lay on a mattress, his thin body in just a grubby singlet and nappy. He had never had his own clothes. Maxine had already learnt that if she bought new clothes for Don they got swallowed up by the laundry and were given to other children.

'Let's get you out of here today, Don.' His face lit up as she settled him on her hip. In the car she changed his nappy and put on the clothes she kept for him, a new t-shirt, windcheater, long pants and socks.

Maxine drove further north-west, following the Derwent River up to Mt Field National Park, the oldest National Park in Tasmania. She spread a blanket on the grassy open ground under the eucalypts by the creek. Maxine squatted down and held Don close to the edge of the creek and they quietly watched a platypus skim just under the surface, its brown body merged with the clear brown creek waters before it ducked under the tree roots on the riverbank.

'It's beautiful, isn't it Don?'

They settled down on the blanket together with pillows to support his bony body. Maxine slowly fed Don the soft food she had prepared, and had a few mouthfuls of her sandwich. Smiling, she felt lucky.

'Can you see the fish up there in the clouds and look, that cloud looks like a dragon.' Maxine glanced over; Don had slipped into a soft sleep. She closed her eyes too.

Later she bundled him up and carried him through the rainforest ferns and dripping trees, the sounds of the waterfall called them on, up the gentle incline and onto the rocks. The glorious cascade tumbled down in front of them. Maxine sat on a large boulder by the water, with Don settled in her lap. She took off her shoes and socks and Don's socks too; he never wore shoes; his pale bare feet rarely touched the earth.

'Would you like to wear shoes, you know like these?' Maxine pointed to her runners. 'Maybe I can get you some.'

Maxine rested both their feet in the cool rocky creek below the tiered waterfall. She wriggled her toes. They laughed.

As Don leant into her, she splashed the water around their feet, swirling patterns between the stones.

Maxine treasured their time together; it was like Don came to life, new breaths with new experiences, flushed cheeks and chuckles, and love. She wanted to give him more and more. Daytime visits and outings just weren't enough. Maxine wished Don could come and stay overnight with her. She wanted to rescue him from the horrors she had seen at Willow Court.

~

It didn't take much when Maxine was little for her blood to pulse fast through her veins, and her eyelids to flicker. She didn't know it was called fear. But eight-year-old Maxine quickly knew that it wasn't a good idea to send little Geoff up to the house and ask for a sweet but too late he had already taken off.

Every week, on a Wednesday Maxine looked out for the big blue, bulky grocery van that travelled Vincent's Road, way up and across the valley. The van never came up her road because they were the last and only house.

'Not worth the petrol,' the driver had told Maxwell.

So instead, someone in the family had to walk up from the steep valley to the drop off point to collect their sugar bag full of groceries. It was usually Maxine and Maxwell together who would tramp up the hill amidst the raspberry and gooseberry canes on her Nan's property at Pelverata. As she hopped across the stream she was always on the lookout for little trout.

Trout loved to have their tummies tickled. Her Dad and Nan taught her how to hover over them as they swam in the cool creek water, to wait patiently as the fish rested on their way upstream to spawn. Just as they took a rest she would gently and slowly place her hand across a trout's back and with extended fingers find their tummy and tickle. She was astounded how they relaxed, still and calm, and then she would gently release her hand and the fish would move on and upwards along the stream.

One day, Maxine didn't go up with her Dad. Colleen wanted her to stay put and keep an eye on Geoff who was four years old. Colleen always asked Maxine to mind him but the task was getting harder as he realised he didn't have to do as he was asked. Sometimes he even pretended that Maxine hurt him. He screamed until Colleen appeared.

'You are not looking after him properly,' she said. There were times when Maxine wanted to hit him but she knew her Mum would hit her harder.

Maxine watched her Dad arrive back with the sugar bag slung over his shoulder and a cigarette in his mouth. He walked up to the house and in through the screen door. Geoff and Maxine were playing under the big gum tree at the end of the driveway. It was hot, dry and dusty.

Most Wednesdays Geoff and Maxine were allowed a penny stick each, a pink, sugary sweet that tasted of musk.

Time went on and Maxine became restless wondering if one of their parents would open the door and ask them to come in for their weekly treat. Usually by now they would be sucking on their lolly, but time ticked by.

'Geoff,' she said, 'go up and ask if we can have our penny stick now.'

He took off at a rate of knots up to the house.

Suddenly there was an almighty bang of the screen door as Colleen lurched out, and even from where Maxine stood under the gum tree, she could see her Mum's eyes. Colleen ran towards Maxine with a huge stick.

'Why don't you do your own dirty work, sending a baby up to ask for lollies.' Maxine ran like she'd never run before, along the driveway, up along the road, all the way Colleen screaming at her, the stick waving. Her heart beat so fast, and she knew the more she ran the more trouble she was in. But if she stopped, she would be beaten.

She turned around and started to run back toward the house, her Mum following.

'Stop, wait till I get hold of you!'

Arriving back at the house breathless, Maxine crashed through the door and into the kitchen where her Dad was sitting by the fireplace.

'Please, make Mum stop,' she pleaded as Colleen thumped her way up the steps to the house and through the door. Maxwell just sat. Colleen grabbed her, threw her toward the bedroom, hitting her as she went. Maxine fell into her bedroom, hitting her head on her metal pram. Blood poured from her eye area. She panicked. Not from the beating (she would normally not cry) but from the terror of knowing her head or eye was cut.

Later when she woke up her right eye wouldn't open, and the bed was covered in blood. Her sobs brought Colleen into her room where she took one look at Maxine and tried to cuddle her, sorry words flowed but Maxine sat cold, still and silent.

A week later, Maxine sat in between her parents, visiting family friends.

'You've been in the wars, girlie.'

'Yes,' said Colleen. 'She fell over.'

Maxine reached her hand to her swollen face and eye, still smarting and smiled, then lowered her eyes and fiddled with her dress hem. She wished then that someone, anyone would take her away.

Chapter 11

It was already late on a cold, wet night while Maxine waited for the Church Minister in the coffee shop in Sandy Bay. A mutual friend suggested he might be a good person to talk with. He was a bit like a counsellor, not that she needed counselling.

She wasn't sure about the Minister bit, *was he going to talk about religion?* But she was battling Willow Court again. She wanted to see more of Don, more than the visits to her childcare centre and occasional visits on weekends, and she needed support, the support of a respected person in the community.

She ordered a coffee and wondered about her own rejected Catholic religion. When she was eleven, she had believed confirmation was sacred. She had stood tall and still in her prickly white dress with long sleeves and puffed out skirt, and long socks. She held white gloves in her clasped hands and looked straight ahead. Her short, light-brown hair sat under a veil that fell in layers down her back. The veil was a 'once only'; she would never wear a wedding veil.

Back then she had liked the local nuns, but not the priests in their stiff robes. When the nuns came for dinner Maxine stayed up and listened intently to their stories. She liked the sound of their independent lives, they were teachers and looked after children, they travelled too, and they helped the poor. The nuns never married. She thought that she might become a nun one day. That was before the accident.

~

New Year's Eve 1968, Maxine was eleven. Her family rented one of the farmhouses in the Huon Valley, beside the river. Seven-year-old Geoff would tease his sisters big and little, then play innocent and race around careless and carefree.

The tomato plants were staked in the veggie patch and the cabbages and silverbeet near the chicken run covered in wire, were looking healthy. A gate enclosed the backyard and opened to the paddocks towards the river.

Big machines were digging a dam down in the paddocks that summer. The children all knew they had to stay within the yard and not climb onto the top of the chicken coop for a bounce on the wire or to watch their Dad with the big diggers.

Inside, the kitchen filled with delicious smells of roast lamb cooking in the electric frying pan. They had picked raspberries for their tea. Geoff was called in, but didn't answer. Colleen called again.

'Go and find him,' Colleen said and Maxine went out into the backyard to look for him. She could hear the chickens clucking. But she had a funny feeling in her chest, something didn't feel right.

Maxine kept calling; she looked in the veggie garden, over past the garage on one side, and a fence on the other. She wondered if he had gone down into the paddocks where the diggers were working. Eventually she climbed up onto the top of the chicken shed where she found him.

He had flesh burns on his face and looked as if he had been thrown backwards. She called Geoff's name then gingerly bent down to touch him. Zap! She clambered down as fast as she could and in between dry sobs and gulping breaths, ran to her Mum.

'Turn off the power, Maxine,' Colleen said. 'And go and find your father. And Sherry, turn the roast down,' she said, words tumbling as she ran outside towards the chicken shed.

Maxine raced down to the paddock. The ground was bumpy and she fell in a hole, scrambled up, panting, with mud splattered everywhere and yelled 'Dad' towards the river.

Later inside they sat on the lounge. Her Mum had tried to revive Geoff. Her Dad was crying. The ambulance came. So did the police. Geoff lay in their parents' bedroom.

Geoff had a little white coffin. It sat up the front of the Sacred Heart Church beneath the tall timber ceiling in Ranelagh. Maxine sat in the front row with her Nans. Her Mum sobbed and her Dad was ghost white. She held herself tightly, hands clasped, back straight, scared and numb at the same time.

She turned, wondering who was behind her and if it was appropriate to wave to familiar faces.

She worried about her little sister too. The priest droned on. She didn't like him or what he was saying. Inside her head she disagreed with him. Outside, in a paddock, were pine trees and horses grazing.

Geoff was buried in the cemetery behind the Church, near the Huon River and not far from home. Other family members were buried nearby. There were visits to the cemetery. At home Maxine's Dad had to continue cutting the hay.

Maybe Maxine's parents could have sued the power company, but who did that in 1960s Tasmania? Certainly not a young working-class family. Their black and white television didn't work well; a maze of wires ran from the house to the wire around the chicken coop. And sometimes they got a mild shock when they turned on the tap in the kitchen.

It was in the papers; Geoff had been electrocuted. The house wasn't properly earthed.

'Why did God let Geoff die?' Maxine asked a priest after the accident.

'If there was no death, there would be too many people,' he said smugly. It wasn't a satisfactory answer.

Soon after, Maxine announced to her mother 'I am not going to church anymore.'

~

The tall, balding man with a round face and glasses finally walked into the coffee shop. He was about fifteen years older than Maxine, and looked conservative in his white shirt and black pants.

He had a limp, the result of childhood polio. He walked towards her, smiling warmly. She was observant and believed that she could make quick and accurate assessments about people.

They introduced themselves. Their conversation started off a little awkwardly but they were soon chatting and Maxine told him about Don.

'I take Don out with me in the car, just to get him out of that horrible place for a few hours. We walk by the river, look at the ducks, cuddle and chat. Sometimes I take him up to Mt Field for a picnic, I love it up there,' she said. The Minister leant forward and rested his face on his hand, as he listened.

'What about the staff there?'

'Hostile. They don't like me; I gave evidence against them at an Inquiry. And they can't understand why I'd want to involve myself with Don.'

Maxine looked down and sipped her coffee.

'The social worker in the department is okay. She helps me to arrange the visits but at times I have Don in my arms, ready to go, and the staff stop me.'

'Why?'

'Oh, they make stuff up, they pretend he is sick, but he seems fine to me.'

The Minister reached over and touched her arm.

'I wish I could just take Don home with me, but I can't,' she said. She looked down at his hand on her arm. 'I only have permission to take him out for a few hours on the weekends.'

The Minister was kind, empathic and enthusiastic. But maybe a little too enthusiastic, she thought. He insisted they go back to her flat in Lower Sandy Bay and they talked on intensely until dawn. Finally, he left and Maxine slept. She felt a little uneasy about him but ignoring that feeling, she let it be. She was so glad he listened and he did seem interested in Don.

Chapter 12

Maxine and the Minister went out for meals and walks together and soon became lovers. She could really talk with him. He encouraged her and supported her to see Don more. Her vitality and ideas must have been exciting to him; she was doing what many in the church just talked about, battling bureaucracy, naming injustice, and caring for Don. Her enthusiasm gave the Minister energy and their time together left her smiling inside.

But he wanted more of her as the months passed, more time, more commitment and she wasn't sure.

She was busy with work and Don, other friends and occasional visits with her own family. Then he said that he wanted to marry her, it was the logical next step.

Marriage! His tenderness was sweet, but she had decided long ago, that she wasn't going to do that. She didn't want to have children, or be a normal parent; she didn't want to do normal. Being a housewife would be boring. She wanted to work, be independent. And although he told her he was separated, he still had a wife and was a Churchman. Maxine didn't want to even think about it, but if their relationship were to continue, they would have to marry eventually. It was an expectation, he couldn't have a long-term lover; he had his family, his parents, his community and the Church to consider.

To harden her feelings and clear her head she escaped to the mainland for a few months. She could close off compartments in herself, but it was easier away from him. She travelled up the east coast into Queensland with a male friend, then back down to Canberra where she lived alone, content in her two-man tent in a caravan park for a few months.

But Tasmania called her back; it was her place. Her lover, the Minister, was still waiting for her; they had exchanged letters. And, of course, she missed Don.

Back in Hobart under the watchful gaze of Kunanyi/Mt Wellington, Maxine was offered her old childcare position at Bridgewater, part-time, and she was asked to establish a new childcare centre in Sorell a few days a week.

She was busy with the responsibilities of these two jobs but also determined to see more of Don. It wasn't unheard of for teachers or staff to become fond of some of the children at Willow Court and, with the misguided notion that they could achieve miracles, take them home for a night or a weekend.

The children's smiles were rewarding and tender moments could melt hearts. Most did it maybe once or twice. Then, faced with the reality of caring for a child with a disability twenty-four hours a day, feeding, changing, engaging, creating activities and supporting while sleep disturbed, they lost interest.

Maxine was different; she was in for the long haul, even if she didn't know it yet. Others around Maxine, like Alison, watched her and remarked, when interviewed, that Maxine showed her fierce commitment. Maxine's approach, in her work and her life was not to simply face a brick wall and logically consider the problem. She barely saw the wall. Many people who come to a brick wall, stop intimidated. Or they attempt to dismantle it, one brick at a time, at a safe pace and then maybe go through and have a look around, knowing they could always come back again.

Maxine barged through, seeing only the goal on the other side as bricks tumbled around her. If there were other people behind the wall, they scrambled to get out of the way as bricks spilled down. She fought for what she believed was right.

'You can't see him today.' The staff still put obstacles in her way when she phoned the ward to arrange to take Don out. 'No, not this weekend Maxine.'

'Why not?' she asked. 'Why can't he come home with me? You know I'll look after him. He loves our picnics and outings.' The more she felt the staff's negative response, their resistance, the more committed she was to go all out.

She arranged to speak with the State Welfare Department, Don's legal guardian.

'I am determined to do it. You can't deny him these experiences, bush picnics, the beach on a sunny warm day. Do you take your children fishing at Salamanca, or off the rocks at Sandy Bay?' They listened. 'Why can't Don do that or have a quiet afternoon and night at home with me? He has the same rights as any other child.'

After what seemed like endless negotiations, months spinning into more months, in July 1981, approval was given. Maxine could take Don into her care for short periods, subject to medical approval from the hospital. Some days she took Don to work with her in Sorell. The other children loved Don being there, they fussed over him, chatted away to him and tucked him up in blankets.

One day the children all made chocolate crackles together. They jostled around the mixing bowl licking their fingers. It wasn't long before the crackles were out of the oven cooling in their little paper homes on the cake rack. The delicious treats cooled enough for the children to break off tiny bits of crispy chocolate.

'Here Don, try this,' one child said and he offered Don a taste. He had never before tasted that rich crunchy delight.

Every time Maxine drove towards New Norfolk, past the black swans gliding along the river, returning Don to Willow Court, she heard the whimpers from him; then his cries. How long could she keep doing this, looking after him at home and then the awful taking him back?

Inside the ward at Willow Court, Don would still be crying as she passed him over to the staff. They would barely acknowledge her and turn away, putting him down on a mattress. As she walked back to her car, Maxine felt numb. She knew what it was like to long for someone to come rescue you.

Chapter 13

'G'day.'

Maxine turned around and her face lit up as she put away toys and cleaned up after the children had left for the day. She hadn't seen her friend Paul for about eighteen months. Their undefined friendship of both closeness and irritation had fractured a while back. They had blundered away from each other and Paul had escaped to the mainland.

Tasmania could become claustrophobic, and the need to get off the island often overwhelmed Tasmanians. But islanders often seek islands and Paul landed on another one, this time off Queensland. Maxine occasionally phoned Paul's Mum and asked when he might be back in Hobart. Their friendship seemed like a rubber band, but was there any elasticity left?

'I asked around when I got back and discovered you were here,' Paul said. He had driven to Sorell straight away, parked outside the community hall, seen the little playground, and went in through the door.

'Tell me about Queensland and life on the island?' Maxine said. 'Probably too hot for me!'

'Yeah, it was great. We all just have to get off Tassie for a time, then we appreciate it more when we come back,' Paul said.

And their chat became easy again. Gradually they revived and deepened their friendship. Paul hadn't met Don yet but he was curious. He had heard the stories of the 'maddies' up the river at Willow Court.

'Can I come up there with you one day?' Paul asked a few months later.

'You mean the State garbage bin? Sure, if you want to.'

So, one Saturday they got into the old orange Telecom van Maxine had recently bought, and drove up to Willow Court to pick up Don. Maxine tried to prepare Paul, but no descriptions were adequate.

He was slammed with disgust, he told her later, and overwhelmed with empathy and sorrow. But those words weren't enough. He felt 'an outpouring of pure love'. And although Maxine was beside him that day, his experience was his own. It wasn't about Don either, not then, that personal connection came later. He simply felt gutted. Now he understood the anger he heard in Maxine's voice. That day, a 'whole heap of things shattered inside', about how people treat each other, basic values, and goodness.

~

1981, the International Year of the Disabled Person came and went. Don turned eight that year and Maxine twenty-four. The global initiative of focusing on people with disabilities wasn't on Maxine's radar. But other strong women with disabilities came together in Canberra and created a groundswell of articulate, potent, proactive advocacy. The women told stories of their restricted experiences and their struggles to have more independent full, rich lives. They explained the inability of the States to create environments where people could have a decent quality of life. Conversations continued and informed both government and community service expectations about what a good life with a disability could genuinely entail.

In early 1982 Don spent regular weekends with Maxine, and Paul often joined them, hanging out and fishing off the wharf at Salamanca. Don, rugged up with a beanie and trackies, warm socks and his own shoes, clasped his own hand line.

If Don felt any movement on the line he yelled and Maxine swung into action, holding Don's arm and leaning across his stroller, she pulled in the line. They tilted their heads back and laughed, winter sun on their faces. They drank tea from their thermos, Don sipping with a cup and straw. Later they wandered around the docks and across the road by the shops at Salamanca.

One weekend, Maxine, Don and Paul headed over to Bruny, the island off the island. They drove south early to the Kettering wharf to catch the old, single-deck car ferry, the Mangana, named after a Chief of the Bruny Island people. Mangana's daughter, Truganini, became the symbol of the struggle for the survival of the Indigenous peoples in Tasmania.

Paul drove onto the Mangana and parked two cars back from the bow. Don was in Maxine arms in the passenger seat. He had never been on the water like this before. The ferry engines throbbed a constant loud rhythm as they moved away from the wharf, a slow movement, gently rolling with a small swell. Don screamed, a piercing scream for the whole forty-minute crossing into Barnes Bay. Other passengers stared at the three of them in their car.

'They must be wondering what we are doing to this poor child,' Maxine looked over at Paul.

'Let them wonder,' he said, with a shrug.

As soon as they drove off the wharf at Barnes Bay Don stopped screaming. He seemed fine. Maxine guessed he had been terrified by the strange movement of being in a car with the engine off, while a different engine throbbed. Being surrounded by, and be crossing over water with other cars and people. By the time they arrived at Paul's family shack on North Bruny, Paul and Maxine were exhausted.

After a weekend of beach walks, playing in the sand, picnics, watching for dolphins and fishing, they were tense as they drove onto the ferry once more. But Don spent the whole trip looking around; he seemed fine now that he had done it before; seemed to be enjoying the experience.

Another Sunday afternoon Maxine and Paul drove by the Derwent River, taking Don back to the institution. When they came to Granton, Don started to whimper. They drove on to the park on the side of the road just outside New Norfolk and by this stage Don was screaming. Maxine knew the horror of Don's screams well, but it was a sound, even worse than on the ferry crossing that Paul had never heard before. Don's whole being seemed to be wrapped up in that sound. Maxine sat; her steely look aimed straight ahead. She felt Paul glance across at her.

'This happens every time, now,' she said, gripping the steering wheel. They drove onto the asphalt – the apron outside Willow Court – and Maxine lifted Don out of the van and carried him inside.

'Ah, here is Don,' a nurse's aide said. Don continued to scream and his arms thrashed about.

'Put him over there on that mattress,' the worker said and walked away. Maxine put him on the floor and once again there was no one, no soft comforting voice, no cuddle.

'See you next time, Don,' Maxine stroked his wet face. She walked away and they drove home in silence.

~

By mid-1982, Don was regularly spending four days a week with Maxine. During the week, with Don beside her again at work, Maxine set up plastic sheets on the floor with little mounds of clay for the children, ready to be plied, pulled and shaped. Don lay on his stomach across a beanbag, arms in front of him with intense concentration as his fingers touched the damp, earthy substance.

The other children chatted with him, shoved some more clammy clay into his hand and wrapped his stiff fingers around it. The clay's odour filled the room and, mouth wide open, Don grinned and groaned his happy groan.

But he was still pale and vulnerable. He had no wheelchair or special equipment. During the day he sat in his stroller amongst the children's cubby houses made with fabric and chairs scraped along the floor. Laughter, shouts and games swirled around him. At rest time Maxine laid him gently on a beanbag, so he could stretch his twisted body.

But after the weekends and weekdays, at some point Don still had to go back to his permanent home at Willow Court. Maxine continued to steel herself on those journeys as she drove alongside the Derwent River.

The screaming would soon start and there was nothing she could do to stop it. The Boyer Paper Mill loomed large on the north bank of the river with a number of chimney stacks billowing fumes. When Don spotted the Mill out of the back window, his screams intensified and did not stop. Exhausted, Don moaned on arrival.

Chapter 14

Maxine and her Minister boyfriend sat in her flat on the eastern shore at Lindisfarne; she had moved house again, near the water overlooking the Derwent Bridge. Maxine was good at creating new homes, like her Mum. She reckoned her Mum and Dad had moved house about ten times in twenty-five years of marriage.

The first thing Maxine and her sister had to do when they arrived at a new home was make the beds and put the kettle on. And if they weren't moving house, and Colleen wanted a change, she moved the rooms around! It was nothing for Maxine to come home and find the lounge room where the main bedroom used to be, and have to hunt down where her bedroom was.

~

Maxine and her boyfriend sipped their cups of tea and chatted about their day. As usual he wore his black pants and neat white shirt. His uniform. He had been held safe within his Church's conservative boundaries and along she came, a free spirit, challenging society's rules, dating both women and men, and fighting bureaucracy. The idea of marriage still hung over them silently. She thought he assumed it would happen, simply done and dusted. Maxine continued to avoid that conversation, and the thoughts of the lifestyle she would be expected to live as a Minister's wife. Not for her. Also, somewhere in the back of her mind, was a niggle. She didn't feel completely safe.

The conversation returned to Don. He was back up at Willow Court and Maxine needed her lover to be the good listener, as he had been when she first met him. He had finally met Don at Willow Court, but had not really spent much time with him. He wasn't keen on the three of them being together.

'You know, the nurses still try and stop him from coming and staying with me,' Maxine said. 'They rang me again at the last-minute last weekend and told me he was too sick to come out. They think it is me who is upsetting him! Can you believe that? He often vomits when I drop him off, his little body heaves and they blame me. I don't know why I take him back to that horrible place at all.'

Don's back-and-forth life was not good for him. She loved caring for him, making him laugh and giving him simple and wonderful nature experiences, music, games, stories and different tastes. He settled more deeply into her heart. She had to make a decision.

But getting someone out of Willow Court would be like busting someone out of prison. Not only that, she would be up against apathy, suspicion and distrust.

'I can't keep doing this; it's not fair on Don,' Maxine said. During her last visit she saw an older child drag a younger one along the floor, like a doll, a whimpering plaything.

'I have fully thought about this. I have to stop bringing him home altogether or look after him full-time. Really there is no choice. I can't leave him there. Would you support me doing this?'

The Minister put his cup of tea down on the table in front of him and looked up at Maxine.

'No way,' he said.

Silence. Maxine waited, tried to stay still. No. She wanted to jump up and leave. In that moment she knew their relationship was over. It seemed like he wanted to look after her, but maybe he didn't want anything that took her attention away from him.

'Okay, I will do it by myself.' *I can do it somehow, just me and this little person I love.*

There was nothing more to say.

~

A short while later she discovered she was pregnant.

'Was it Paul, or that friend that you travelled with on the mainland?' the Minister asked.

'Don't be ridiculous, you know they are both just friends,' she said.

She arranged a termination. He gave her some money. Many years later Maxine realised it was very wrong that they were ever lovers. But it was good he hadn't supported her decision to look after Don full-time. It would have been disastrous to bring Don into that relationship.

~

Maxine broached the subject of adoption with her Mum. The family had met Don several times when he was with her on weekends. Maxine's sister Sherry knew him a little better than the others; she met Don when she helped out at the childcare centre at Sorell and occasionally did the weekend drive with Maxine up to New Norfolk. Sherry understood Maxine's fierce protectiveness.

Colleen thought that Don was the cutest little thing, and she understood that Maxine didn't want her own children.

'Don't be stupid, you'll ruin your life,' Colleen said in her straightforward way.

But there would be no stopping Maxine. Her mother knew that too.

Chapter 15

Maxine had to find her way around a complex welfare system. Both fostering and adoption carried legal and bureaucratic weight, and social meaning.

Adoption was permanent, the new parents totally responsible for their precious child. Couples usually adopted children when they were unable to have their own. Maxine certainly knew she was fertile.

Fostering was temporary and carried less responsibility. Not that Maxine was afraid of responsibility or commitment. Foster parents at that time were often working-class people, and fostering wasn't necessarily respected. During the 1950s, 60s and early 70s some parents fostered children to supplement a family's low income and to open their homes to less advantaged children.

Maxine's own parents had done this, taking in a baby for a short while, and later a young boy lived with them for many months.

But Maxine didn't need extra money, she was only thinking about how she could care for Don full-time. Her focus was Don's needs. She had her own career and was earning her own money. And always would.

There were rumours; Maxine heard the whisperings around Hobart. Yes, her sexuality was ambiguous, (she was weird, was she a lesbian)? And she had had an affair with a Minister of religion, who was separated but still married (she was definitely a home wrecker). The various rumours didn't quite add up but she was clearly not a 'nice, stable, married woman'. Not an ideal candidate as an adoptive or foster parent.

Maxine had already tried to negotiate with the authorities to put Don into Quindalup Respite Centre four nights a week where he could attend the day training centre away from Willow Court. *At least he might learn something there!* Then, Don could be with her the rest of the time, at work and at home. But that wasn't possible, the Centre catered for short respite not ongoing care and its focus and service would soon be changing. Full-time care with Maxine was the only option.

'You know he's extremely distressed every time he goes back to Willow Court.' Maxine kept telling the authorities. 'It is traumatic for him, more added trauma each time in his short life! And lots of the staff there do not want him staying with me anymore. They make it so hard for him. It is completely unfair on Don.'

~

One sunny Sunday Maxine thought about her own childhood as she guided Don around in his stroller, along the waterfront at Sandy Bay, looking out at the yachts and across the river to the eastern suburbs and the dry rounded hills.

Maxine's family had been poor, with few books and material possessions, but rich with farm produce, jobs and acres to explore and play in. She liked being on the swing in the backyard, but didn't like to be pushed too high; not quite trusting what would happen. She liked to propel herself, go at her own pace in her own time and still enjoy the ride.

Her favourite activity was sitting on a tree trunk, high up and looking out beyond the Huon River nearby. When she reminisced, Maxine remembered the good parts of her childhood and rarely thought of the other.

When Maxine was in Grade 1 at school, the family lived in a house surrounded by paddocks. Even then she treasured her independence. She made her own lunch and got ready by herself. She put on her short blue socks, though they accentuated her skinny bruised shins and slipped on her polished black shoes. She loved walking through the rough grass up to the bus stop, climbing over the fence, even on cold frosty mornings, and stepping into icy puddles that crackled underfoot. In spring the hardened winds eased making way for the bulbs to raise their delicate faces to the sun.

As a child, when outside with her Dad Maxine dressed in overalls, like a boy. She rode with him on the tractor around the farm; sometimes he even let her drive. Her thin legs were long but she still had to stand up to reach the pedals and hold on tightly to the large heavy steering wheel.

Inside the house Maxine wore little pinafore dresses overlaid with checked aprons bought by her Nan, Edith. Edith's favourite outfit was her olive-green coat with fake fur, adorned with an emerald-green brooch, and hat and stockings. She always wore her stockings, even when she paddled in the water with her shoes off, on a hot Hobart family beach day.

'You have to play in the backyard if you're just in your shorts,' her Mum said when Maxine was older. She loved being outside, after the spring winds that roared around the island had gone, when summer glided back in, bleaching the sky.

'Why should I?' Maxine didn't like the idea of putting on a shirt.

'You can't be in the front yard with no top on,' her Mum said. There were budding breasts starting to show; Maxine didn't want those. She felt neither a boy nor a girl back then. She was a ladylike tomboy.

When the crisp mornings of autumn came around again with glorious sunny deep blue days that slipped quietly into cold, Maxine collected kindling for the fire and watched her Dad chop wood out the back. She loved being with her Dad then and when he drove trucks.

~

Maxine felt sad for Don as she guided him along the path by the beach. He had no swings or school, no delicious roast lamb, no homework or holidays, no wooden trucks, or drives with a father in real trucks, no game of cards or bits of Monopoly strewn around on the floor. And no sweet smell of juicy apples filling the packing shed as the whole family chipped in, working hard in the sheds down the Huon Valley. The crisp shiny apples were sorted and the wooden crates were loaded and trucked into Hobart.

Conversations always flew across the wide-open shed while Maxine looked out across red and green acres of apple trees, some varieties still laden with fruit, ready to be picked. The Golden Delicious crop settled in the cardboard bins. It was a dreamy and busy time all mixed together as the vitality of the fruit seeped into the air and the rhythm and repetition of the packing soothed the rough edges of other days.

Apple time was extra special. Each year Maxine sat with her Dad in the cab of the truck, as it trundled from the Huon Valley up into town and down Davey Street towards the docks for shipping. Just her and her Dad, chatty above the engine rumble and then quiet, content, together.

If she had been a boy, she could have been with her Dad longer in the trucks and the other truckies' language would not have been a problem. She wouldn't have had those looks; those looks that made her feel uncomfortable.

In the evenings when her Mum, the great aunties and her other grandmother, Pearl, were together there was always laughter around the table. The meal over, it would be time for a cup of tea and a yarn. Her Mum would swivel herself around, cross one leg over the other, light a cigarette and get comfortable and ready. Maxine kept quiet, with her long thin legs tucked up underneath her. She was allowed to sit with the older women as they drank cups of tea and, invisible again, she watched and listened; absorbing the banter and stories.

'Remember the overalls you used to wear, Colleen, with sticks and stones stuffed into your pockets?' the eldest aunty said to Maxine's Mum, one night. 'You were a spirited tomboy with your hair tucked away in plaits and your pet wombat. And you taught maths to the chooks out the back.' Chuckles babbled around the table.

'And when I started to grow out of my favourite overalls, Mum stitched pieces of fabric onto the ends of the legs. Colleen said. 'You taught us well, Mum. We all learnt to make do.'

Don was missing out on so much. There were no fights with a brother or sister, no knowing looks between them, or tired parents or arguments. No aunties and no grandparents. For Don there was no privacy, not even a room, just a ward full of cots against walls. Maxine knew that many children died in institutions all around Australia. *Why would they want to live? What did they have to look forward to? What might they hope for?*

Maxine and Don sat in the sun beside the brick wall, sheltering from the wind, looking across Sandy Bay beach.

'What a beautiful day, Don,' Maxine said taking off his beanie and ruffling his hair. Other families walked past, around the point and onto the next little beach. Some smiled as they passed, others looked away.

'What's wrong with him?' a child asked.

'Nothing,' Maxine replied too quickly, as she held a drink with a straw to Don's mouth. But there was a lot wrong with his life. He needed a home.

~

Although Maxine was now recognised as an informal part-time foster carer of Don, she had to find more stable accommodation than the schoolhouse in Sorell where she was living, if she wanted to have Don with her full-time. She and Paul were spending more time together and talked about jointly renting a house. Maxine informed the Department she was looking to rent a home with a friend. Paul was around because of his friendship with her, not because of Don. They could make it work.

One social worker recognised Maxine's beneficial relationship with Don and her care of him, including being aware of his health risks. Maxine had been taught some simple physiotherapy. She would pat his back as he was lying over a bean bag to help Don with his lack of resistance to chest infections. The worker also reasoned that the success of Maxine's full-time care of Don would only be proved or disproved by experiment and that Maxine should be given the opportunity to prove she could cope with caring for Don as long as he did not suffer in any way.

Other people, officials in the Department, were concerned

that Maxine was spending more and more time with Don and talking about fostering him possibly at the expense of her own life opportunities.

It needed very careful consideration; it would not be a hurried decision. They were not sure about the feasibility of Don living in a normal home environment in the community. How would his needs be 'serviced?'

The Director noted that he did not want to see her extend herself beyond her current commitment to Don. She kept going regardless.

She had made her decision and didn't even think about their concerns. Communication between the hospital, the ward and the Department and Maxine was slow, arrangements were unclear, and recommendations made, but not communicated well or not yet acted upon. She was waiting for a decision about permanent care.

In November 1982 Maxine returned Don to M ward once again. As usual Don was screaming in her arms as she entered the building, and in that moment, she simply walked back out with him. She could not leave him there again.

Part Two

Creating homes

Risks, adventures and advocacy

Chapter 16

A month later in December 1982, Maxine and Paul found a large, airy home in Elphinstone Road, Mount Stuart, a hilly suburb hugging the foothills of Kunanyi/Mt Wellington. The high-set redbrick house had concrete steps leading up to the front door. Paul's room was at the front. Maxine's was out the back, beside the little room she set up for Don, overlooking the bushy garden.

A trial period of full-time fostering began, but she lived with the constant threat that Don could be taken back into Willow Court at Royal Derwent Hospital if the trial was unsuccessful.

One morning, Don woke, about seven, with his usual groan. Maxine wondered if he was still getting used to sleeping alone. He wasn't used to his cries bringing someone. Maxine appeared at his door.

'How did you sleep, Don? Okay, let's get you changed and ready for the day.' He needed a sponge down in the morning, a change of nappy and a fresh singlet. That cold morning was a December day when summer and winter temperatures teased.

Maxine carried Don into the living room, laid out his clothes on the couch, new clothes – comfy but not cheap: tracky pants, t-shirt, warm pale green windcheater, and thick socks.

His legs were awkward to dress. Maxine would bunch up

a leg of his pants and pull one foot through then the other, then push the pants up his legs, lean further over and lift his bottom and pull up his tracky pants. When his arms and legs stiffened with spasms unexpectedly, or were floppy, they were hard to manoeuvre. If he spasmed when getting his shirt and jumper on, Maxine could collect a whack on the arm or in the face.

Don might have wanted to help himself get dressed, but he couldn't. The commands to his body didn't register. But over time getting dressed became quicker and easier.

'Okay, one arm now, Don.'

His brown hair flopped down his forehead and he grunted.

Maxine smiled.

'Do you like this new jumper? So much nicer than those huge, old, sloppy hand-knitted things.'

Maxine lifted Don, buckling him into his stroller. She had a quick shower and got dressed.

'A wheelchair would be great, Don.' Willow Court had never provided Don with any equipment. 'We will have to sort out that next.' Don grinned.

In their new home, Maxine stepped into a more settled phase in her life. She soon began running family daycare, play sessions in her big L-shaped living room with Don and some local children and, in another integration first, some were children with disabilities. Her previous integration had been successful when Maxine managed the childcare centre in Bridgewater.

In the late afternoons in the back garden Maxine gathered the garden hose and with Don leaning into her in a standing position, she held one arm around his waist and the other across his shoulder and chest. She strung the hose over both their shoulders and they watered the plants together. Don liked to try and stand at other times too, resting a little weight on Maxine's feet while she held his body as straight as she could and walked a few steps.

On hot Hobart days Maxine laid out a small, blue, plastic wading pool on a larger mattress. Don, his limbs free in the water, his body briefly liberated, could kick, bump and splash without hurting himself.

~

One of the many cold summer mornings, pulling the blankets around her face, Maxine woke, looked out through the gaps in the curtain, and found slivers of blue and grey.

She hoped it might fine up. She snuggled under the covers for a few more moments knowing, that soon there would be a muffled shout. As usual Paul was fast asleep after working a late shift at the pub.

Don's congested breathing, loud in the next room, meant a quick exit from bed. Maxine shrugged off the blankets, pulled on some clothes, ran her fingers through her short hair and went to him. He moaned and gave her his morning grin. She had to get herself and Don dressed, ready and fed. Maxine had started to explore what activities and services were available for Don in the community. There had to be some if he was going to live with her permanently.

Today, David Bowling, the paediatric social worker at Douglas Parker Rehabilitation Centre in Hobart, was coming.

His employer – the government service for children and adults with physical disabilities – ran the centre which offered various therapies and focused on physical rehabilitation. It also had a special school, the D'alton School, on site.

David, tall and thin, with a quiet measured voice, and a

thoughtful presence, was one of a new breed of enthusiastic young social workers, questioning conventional ways of doing things. He had a lightness about him. Maxine sensed both movement and stillness.

David was often the first member of the Departmental assessment team families met and, with his social work role, he did assessments and home visits. He was also keen to talk families through the complicated process of rehabilitation at Douglas Parker.

When she had first met David, Maxine had worn her usual jeans and a t-shirt. She didn't dress up for professionals. Yet she had an unusual request of him.

Maxine's request for community services was uncommon as Don was still, officially, a patient at Willow Court and the Douglas Parker Centre didn't support those children. Maxine, however, persisted and managed to persuade David to agree to at least an assessment.

When David arrived to meet Don, she led him out to the back garden where she had laid out rugs. The early cloud had burnt off leaving a warm sunny day.

Don lay on a mat and on either side of his body, had sandbags weighing him down in an attempt to decrease his muscle spasms.

'A therapist's idea,' Maxine said indicating the beanbags full of sand. Don could stay flat on the beanbag on his tummy and use his arms to play. 'I make them out of pillowcases with sand at either end.'

'You look comfortable there, Don,' David said. He settled himself on the ground and talked with Don the same way he might have talked to any other nine-year-old.

Don's diagnoses at that time: profound visual and intellectual impairment in addition to his physical handicaps were significant but David thought Don was old enough to have it all explained to him.

'We are looking into what may be available for you Don, like going to school, going swimming in our therapy pool. Do you like swimming?' Don kept looking at David while he talked.

'There are communication aids too that might help you, so you can tell us what you like and don't like.' David was careful to explain the centre's activities including the fact that Don would meet various people with whom he might be able to do a variety of things.

'That went well,' Maxine said after David left, and picked Don up.

She carried him inside and laid him on the bed. His turned his head and looked away, his back arched. He groaned. Maxine smiled at his small ways of asserting himself.

It was a start. Maxine was sceptical about most of the professionals she met, yet she liked many things about David. He had, at least listened to her; he had also talked directly with Don and demonstrated that he had some sense of 'knowing' about Don. Maxine recognised what felt as some agency or capacity in David that she couldn't immediately define, but it was familiar. Something about this encounter resonated and reassured her.

This has to work, she thought. If Don was going to live with Maxine, he had to also have a full, safe and meaningful life out in the community. There had to be support for him, not only from her, but also education, fun, and other loving people who would really care about him.

Maxine felt that finally, people were going to do the right thing by Don. David was going to help. And his daughter was coming to Maxine's playgroup the following day. Don would get to meet her too.

The small weekly playgroup Maxine established at home was going well. Don and a bunch of kids, both 'able bodied' and 'disabled' children, played and did activities together. Compared with some of the 'normal kids', Maxine thought Don was an angel; he was cooperative and happy. She was fed up with the labels these children were landed with. *Stupid labels, they were all crap anyway, who cares?* she thought.

'We are who we are,' she said after the playgroup children had left. Don grinned at her. Maxine put Don into his stroller and took him into the kitchen to prepare his lunch. She warmed leftovers from last night's favourite vegetable casserole. She wasn't hungry. She would mash it with a fork and feed him. If others ever tried to feed him it was a slow drawn-out process, but Maxine managed it quite quickly.

A few days later, David phoned her to arrange assessments for Don with the other therapists at Douglas Parker. The Centre was located in a large, long, hospital-like building, at least three storeys high and much taller than the surrounding houses in the semi-industrial area north of Hobart.

Maxine drove there and once parked, pushed Don in his stroller up to the large doors and into the echoey entrance area. It was draughty, the building forbidding. They met various therapists who assessed Don's capacities.

Yet, Maxine thought that the tests that Don was submitted to were juvenile, too simple.

After all the assessments were done at Douglas Parker, the therapists had a case meeting where David reported his observations to the team.

'He sustained meaningful eye contact with me,' David said.

'He didn't look me in the eye, David,' one therapist said.

'Donald didn't cooperate with me,' said another.

'No, I don't think he is appropriate for Douglas Parker,' another of the therapists said, 'because kids have to have a certain level of intelligence.' All of the others agreed. None had been able to maintain any eye contact with Don and all took that as indicative of his level of intellectual impairment.

'I met Don in completely different circumstances,' David said. 'Don was lying in his backyard, in a safe environment with Maxine nearby, and he sustained meaningful and lengthy eye contact with me as we chatted.'

David argued Don's case with his coworkers. 'Your observations were based on seeing Don in an environment where he was not able to develop a trust relationship with you,' David said.

He was convinced that Don understood what was being said to him. Then, in his firm measured voice, added, 'Are you calling me a liar?'

'No, no we are not doing that.' They were each keen to reassure him.

David managed to convince the team that Don was owed the benefit of the doubt. In light of this, they agreed that Don could come to Douglas Parker on a trial basis.

Don's life was on trial.

Chapter 17

In January 1983 Maxine, Don and a few friends went on a ten-day camping trip to the Tasman Peninsula. Don swam in shallow sheltered beaches, further strengthening his unused muscles and surprising Maxine by keeping himself afloat with only a little support.

On her own precious childhood holidays the family had stayed in shacks at Cockle Creek in the far south of Tasmania, where her Mum's family owned a ninety-year lease. It was the last place with habitation before the southwest wilderness and it was the site of many happy memories of those times.

She tried to give Don some of those happy times when she went collecting shells, paddling, fishing, and wandering.

The young Maxine had disappeared for hours on the beaches, clambered over the colourful rocks, watched the creatures in the pools, the crabs and limpets, tiny darting fish and seaweeds. These young wanderings and independence had helped Maxine develop a sense of her own strengths.

She definitely didn't like the snakes that slithered across bush tracks but still she felt deliciously free. In the evenings, she would join the family and squat down around the campfire, watching the flickering firelight and shadows. She felt safe outside in the dark beside her maternal grandmother. Her Nanna's hands – wrinkled, black and spotty, with fingers stained from smoking – were the ones to hold hers tight when yells erupted from the kitchen, louder and louder, as crockery smashed and forks flew. Those hands protected. Now it was Maxine's turn to be the protector, to keep Don safe.

Don joined a holiday program at Quindalup that January and went on excursions to the airport, the beach and children's playgrounds. He sometimes whimpered and cried when Maxine dropped him off, already missing her, but always grinned and hollered in delight when Maxine picked him up.

With his new experiences, stimulation, and communication with other children and adults especially Maxine, Don's childhood development naturally progressed. When he was nearly seven, he was not given much hope of living past eight! At nine, he was past the pessimistic prognosis made in 1980. In Maxine's care he had managed to develop a high degree of immunity to his previously constant and life-threatening respiratory infections and steadily gained weight.

Don now routinely responded when he heard his name. He could anticipate events from verbal cues, look at pictures, recognise objects when named, and vocalise pleasure and discomfort. With Maxine he loved exploring objects by feeling and rubbing the different textures and enjoyed a range of new sensory activities with new foods and music; he played in sand, water, with play dough and did finger painting.

He greeted familiar people and tried to make himself understood with sounds and facial expressions. He even showed frustration. All of these changes gave Maxine more confidence that she was right; he was intelligent, not 'retarded'.

The assessment team held various case conferences and yet the final decision about permanent care limped on. They agreed Don was doing well. Maxine had been committed to Don since 1978 and her recent part-time care and now full-time was acknowledged. But any certainty about next steps was still complicated by differences in their understandings of categories, legislation and bureaucracy.

A few months went by and in February, there was still no decision.

'Just checking the water,' Maxine called out to Don as she ran the bath for him one evening. She ran her hands through the hot water, added some cold and swished it around. By the time she had undressed Don it should be just right. Don was in the living room lying on a beanbag and Paul had been briefly in and out in the evening and borrowed her van again. She returned to the living room.

'Okay, Don, bath time.'

She lifted him up, carried him to the new change table, a frame with a cloth designed for babies, not children with cerebral palsy. He wriggled. She retracted the sleeve of his jumper from one arm, then the other, and pulled it over his head. His arms were floppy.

'Pants now,' she said. She lifted his bottom and pulled his pants to his thighs, then pulled them off, one leg, then the other. She sat him up for a moment, but suddenly he slipped through her arms and as he fell, caught his leg on the cross bar. Maxine heard the crack. Don screamed.

Oh God, is his leg broken?

Maxine gently disentangled his limbs and lifted him off the change table and onto the couch. His lower leg didn't look right.

Don screamed some more. His face was pale and tight. *Hospital, the van, bloody Paul.* Maxine ran into the kitchen and phoned a taxi.

'Sorry Don, we have to go to hospital.'

She held Don's hand as she snatched the blanket from the back of the couch and covered him. The taxi seemed to take forever and she would have to, somehow, carry him down the front steps when it eventually arrived.

When she heard it arrive, Maxine grabbed her keys and wallet, opened the front door and, gently, carried Don. She managed to pull the door shut behind her. She was conscious that each step down would be jolting his broken bone.

'It's okay, Don. It will all be okay.'

The taxi driver opened the back door and awkwardly she and Don slid onto the back seat. Don lay across her lap for the short trip into the Royal Hobart Hospital and continued to howl. Maxine stroked his hair. *What a nightmare.* She hadn't wanted Don to go near a hospital ever again, after Willow Court. This was their first trip to emergency in her care.

'You right love?' The driver asked.

'I think it's his leg ... broken,' Maxine said.

'Fast as I can,' he said.

They waited in the emergency department. Don whimpered, was quiet, then yelled again. Maxine tried to find a comfortable way to hold him but there was none. The seats were hard plastic.

She looked around – there were many others, anxious, in pain, sick, waiting. She had to repeatedly urge the woman on duty to get a nurse to see Don immediately.

Eventually, a doctor examined Don. Maxine watched him run his eyes down Don's body and legs. *This will be bloody useless.*

They won't have any idea about cerebral palsy; they won't know what to do. They have probably not met a boy like Don here.

The children had all been locked away up the river, not coming into Accident and Emergency with broken bones. They gave Don an injection to calm him down and help with the pain. Then the discussion started. With his condition, with his spasms, they weren't sure if they could plaster his broken leg.

Maxine phoned home. Paul didn't answer. Where was he? She was furious. She was on her own in hospital with Don and without her van. Despite his spasms, they managed to put a plaster cast on his leg, but Maxine wasn't sure if that was going to work, if the plaster would be okay and if his bone could heal when he spasmed and how Don would tolerate the cast. She stayed the night with Don at the hospital, and the following morning took another taxi home. His bathwater was, inevitably, cold.

Maxine had to notify the Department about having to go to Accident and Emergency, and request that she continue to care for Don while he recovered, due to his pain and trauma and ongoing need to attend the fracture clinic. The Department noted it was an accident while Don was being changed. Generally, the placement with Maxine was supported but his progress was being monitored.

Maxine was still waiting for notification of full-time foster care. *Would this jeopardise her chances?*

Chapter 18

'Where is the permanent care process up to?' Maxine asked Departmental staff yet again. 'Are there any barriers? What do I need to do?' She was articulate and persistent, respected by some but her assertiveness was challenging for others. 'And what are you doing to hurry this up?'

Now twenty-five-years-old, Maxine was still battling to dig nine-year-old Don permanently out of his institutional life. She wasn't interested in the details; she just wanted a decision. But it was complex. The most formal way to care for Don full-time, was for the State who acted 'in loco parentis' as a normal reasonable parent for a declared Ward of the State, to delegate that authority to an approved foster carer.

Another was adoption, and this meant a formal legal process with many documents.

The Department recognised that Maxine was 'already caring for' Don for a couple of years. She had been taking Don to work with her, then home while in various childcare positions. She had created a role for herself that was crucial in the process. She had become an 'approved person' for caring. She had, unwittingly, been doing what she was doing without filling in endless official forms.

Permanent Placement with a foster carer and adoption were

very close in terms of legal status, but under Permanent Placement, the Director of Community Welfare made the final decision and they, not the foster carer, remained the legal guardian.

With adoption the State was limited in its support. Apart from formal fostering and legal adoption there was a middle way where a person simply provided temporary care for a child whilst other long-term decisions were made. The State, as legal guardian, maintained an overall responsibility.

There was, also, a space between the State having no role and the State having total responsibility. This was the de facto situation Maxine found herself in with Don. This status had been common during the war years, when parents may have had difficulty caring for their families. It was relatively unusual by the 1980s and it still grappled with the critical issue about what happened when a child turned eighteen.

What Maxine didn't know, alongside these complicated legal classifications, was that there were bureaucrats who realised government policies and services had to change. She had unknown allies in Hobart, supporting her, particularly in the Department of Community Welfare.

The Department was often dragged along, but the small cluster of people, mostly young, social work trained, intelligent, warm-hearted men were slowly working towards social change; at least they were talking about it. They saw that the heavy-handed paternalistic medical institutional model of care wasn't going to survive and that a community-based model was waiting to be developed and implemented. And along came Maxine.

Her innate understanding about integration was obvious. Some bureaucrats were willing to take a stand alongside her, to step out of their defined professional boundaries and support her.

They had the theory and an academic, professional language to describe what Maxine was seeking to do; give Don a life that every child deserved. Maxine was living the theory and was also a fast learner. It was time to pick up the jargon too.

For Maxine to trust anyone was never easy, but she had grown to trust David Bowling, the social worker at Douglas Parker, and Alison Jacob, the School Principal at Willow Court. She then met another David, a social worker in the Department. He was also tall and quietly spoken, with a warm presence. Everything about him felt like he had time and was in control, not in a rigid way, but relaxed.

He understood what Maxine was trying to do and that it was about much more than her and Don, it was about getting governments and communities to think differently about vulnerable people generally and people with a disability in particular. It was certainly not a common conversation at that time.

He and Maxine were able to recognise the overlay of very old-school thinking and then translate ideas into contemporary thinking and potential practices. *Practices!* Maxine only wanted the best life that Don could have.

She couldn't believe the whole 'normalisation stuff' as she called it. Normalisation was a theory that urged services to offer so-called normal and age-appropriate experiences to people with disabilities, social and cultural experiences that allowed them to take risks rather than be forever protected. *Common sense*, she thought. *And people go and study that?*

While these conversations were swirling, Maxine was waiting for a decision and Don's day-to-day life carried on.

'We might go up there,' she told Don one day as they wound along Sandy Bay Road overlooking the water at Taroona, driving past the Shot Tower. She was young and fit, could still carry Don and always wanted to give him new experiences.

She piggy-backed him up the narrow stairs to the top of the tower where the workers used to make the lead shot for guns. It was an awkward piggy-back for them both.

Maxine held Don's arms straight, his knees spasmed into her back but that was the only way they could do it. Don didn't like it, he groaned and cried out. It was probably boring for him, there was nothing really there, and he wanted to come back down. She felt a great sense of achievement for herself, carrying him up there. So, they bumped their way down. She had to sit on her bottom and have Don on her knee. It was the best part for Don as his laughter and yelps echoed around all the long way down.

On other days they ventured over the Pittwater estuary to Wattle Hill, and Paul's parents' farm Dellwood, near Sorell, one of Tasmania's oldest farming communities. Don loved his rides on the buggy, herding up the cows and riding over the bumps. Later, their big black Labrador, the failed seeing-eye dog, joined them too and ran alongside while Maxine held onto Don on the back of the buggy.

Weeks passed. There wasn't a day that qualified as the definite day when Don arrived from Willow Court to live with Maxine permanently, legally fostered with his own possessions. But he didn't have any personal possessions anyway, just smelly other-people's communal clothes, sometimes labelled with another child's name. They were always too big, dreadful, and fell off.

'You have to sort this out; it's taking too long.' Maxine rang the Department yet again. 'You know he is never going back!' Another month passed.

'You can call the police. I am keeping him.'

Chapter 19

There was a knock on the door at Mt Stuart. Maxine checked Don was okay lying on his beanbag on the floor, with books and matchbox cars in front of him. He could swing his arm, with a clenched hand and push his cars along in one direction, with a yelp. His open book with pictures of cars lay there too.

'Look who is here Don, you remember David Bowling,' said Maxine. 'No more home visits, he's here to celebrate with us!'

Success was theirs. In a new guardianship review meeting Maxine's consistent and enriching time with Don was acknowledged, along with the encouraging personal development, and the importance of her significant caring relationship for him. Don was well placed with Maxine; the trial period had been successful.

The criteria normally applied to fostering was not appropriate, Don's placement with Maxine was thought of 'a type of special contract care, without emphasis on contract'.

On 10 March 1983 Maxine was recognised as the person to foster Don on a full-time basis. Don was finally discharged from Royal Derwent Hospital! He was nine years old and Maxine twenty-five.

David had arrived with a gift and he passed it to Don. Maxine helped Don rip off the wrapping paper and unroll a poster for his bedroom wall.

Maxine does not remember ever receiving a formal letter; most of the negotiations had taken place verbally. She had been parenting Don for a long time; it was just normal for them both. At last, after all her bureaucratic battles Don could now legally stay with her.

Maxine could have adopted Don. She thought the Department would have loved that, as their responsibility for him would have completely ceased and she would have been totally responsible for him both as a child and as an adult. But she was very clear. If she had adopted him, she would have been like all the other parents of children with disabilities, the many parents who still placed their children into Willow Court or left them outside Parliament House because they couldn't get the community support they needed. When Don turned eighteen, he would be a totally dependent young adult, with few services for him. *That is not going to happen.* It would not be good for Don and it would not be good for Maxine.

A small fortnightly payment was made to full-time foster parents, not that Maxine needed their money. But the payment did help with Don's clothes and that was fair after all he had been through; he was legally still a Ward of the State.

Despite Maxine's extensive research, there were very few community services available for Don; he was perceived as far too disabled, so once more Maxine had to lobby and create possibilities for him.

She became the Coordinator of Family Day Care for Hobart City Council and in another first, established a Family Day Care program that could take children with special needs into their own homes. Don, of course, was the first one.

He went to the carer's home every day after attending Quindalup, the small daycare and training centre for children with disabilities who were not eligible to go to school.

In a strange twist, Quindalup offered their services on the same grounds of the old Mothercraft home in Newtown. The bus took him there in the mornings and in the afternoons to his family day carer.

Don had put on weight with Maxine's care and home-cooked meals. He had grown out of his little stroller. Her old station wagon had a child seat in the back for him but it was a struggle lifting him in and out and twisting to place him in his seat. Finally, Maxine had acquired a little fold-up wheelchair for Don and, having taken out a personal loan, upgraded to another van.

After work, Maxine arrived at Don's family daycare house. She liked it; the well looked after garden and sense of permanence.

The Mum there had cats and a dog, an eleven-year-old daughter and her elderly father lived there, too.

When the woman opened the door, there was Don in the living room grinning. He threw his head back. He was sitting in his brown fold-up wheelchair, ready for home, his bag beside him. A couple of other children were playing with trains on the floor.

'Have you had a good day, Don?' Maxine asked.

'Yep, we've had a great afternoon.' The carer said. 'Don was quiet when the bus dropped him off, but we had fun,' she turned towards Don.

'Haven't we, Don?' But Don had turned his head away. His Maxine was here now. 'Don helped me water the garden and we fed the cat. And the boys have played with the train set.'

'Great,' said Maxine. 'Thank you. See you tomorrow.'

'Okay let's get home now, Don.'

Maxine wheeled Don out to the van. At that time, a van with a hoist, a set-up disability van wasn't available. So, Maxine negotiated with the Department.

'I've bought the van; you can pay for the hoist. I'll organise to get it made,' she said.

'There is no money available for that; there are no allocated funds,' was the familiar response. They had no funds for 'extra' things that Don needed, including a plastic-moulded chair to be fitted into a wheelchair frame. There was no precedent for such purchases.

'That is not my problem, you are his legal guardian,' Maxine said. 'I am already doing more than my fair share here.'

Maxine learnt that in such departments there were little bits of money – slush funds – money here and there, often unexpended on other projects. She found a welder who built a hoist in the back of the old van so that Don could sit in his wheelchair strapped into the back. Eventually, the Department agreed to pay for the welder and the hoist.

In the back, Don was vocal; his groans were his voice, not a complaint. His left hand twisted inwards and his right arm flew out. He smiled a wide mouth grin.

Maxine climbed into the driver's seat, pulled her seatbelt on and they set off home. 'Paul will be out tonight, I think, so it's you and me. Are you hungry? We can have last night's leftover moussaka.' She chatted on for a while and then was quiet.

'It's big, Don,' she said over her shoulder, 'what we are doing is big.'

Another first, Don at family daycare and it had worked. *More integration, other children will follow.* She smiled as she glanced at Don in the rearview mirror.

They pulled up in the Mt Stuart driveway and stopped in front of the garage. To their right were the eight concrete steps with a white metal railing that lead up to the front door. Maxine climbed out of the driver's seat and headed up the steps.

'Just unlocking the front door, Don.' She ran back down and opened the back of the van, wheeled Don out, then lifted him into her arms and carried him up. She didn't have the energy that day to pick up the chair with Don in it and carry him up the steps. She did that when she was in a hurry; it was quicker but heavier. Inside the house was cold. She put on the electric heater.

'We need a warmer house, Don. Just for you and me. And we need to find you a proper school.'

She laid Don down on the couch in the living room and went back down to grab the bag of shopping she had bought at lunchtime, as well as the wheelchair. Don called out from upstairs.

'Coming, Don,' she ran back up the steps.

In the kitchen she poured herself a whiskey and began reheating the food.

Chapter 20

A proper education for Don was the next priority. Maxine didn't want him to just attend Quindalup, as its primary focus was to support children with intellectual disabilities. Don's disability was physical. Sometimes he had been left sitting in extreme discomfort, unchanged for long periods and there were two accidents over two years, another leg injury and a fall from a toilet chair. Maxine believed that Don understood more than his peers at Quindalup. She wanted an environment where he could reach his full potential, a fundamental right of every child. And she didn't want to waste any more time!

Maxine's own schooling had started late and was interrupted. When she was little the family had stayed at her Nan's place in Pelverata, one of the narrow valleys in the bush south of Hobart when her Dad was out of work. One day when she was about seven, an official from the education department arrived at the house.

'This girl should be at school by now,' the official said. The little adult inside Maxine agreed with the official. *Yes, this is right. I should be at school.* She knew other children went to school.

To ensure she could go to school, the family had to move house again – they didn't have a car to get her to school from Pelverata. It was her fault, some of the family thought. She thought, *good.*

'You don't have to come in with me,' Maxine said to her mother when they arrived at school on her first day. It was exciting to be going to kindergarten, getting away from home, but a little scary. Her whole body lit up inside.

~

As Maxine researched educational options for Don, she was pushed from one place to another because of internal politics that meant no one was taking responsibility. She discovered there was no legal requirement for him to go to school; the Education Department had no obligation to teach children like Don, as he was 'too handicapped'. What was the point of educating children like Don? It even seemed to be illegal for Don to go to school.

'Imagine if your child had years of life without a loving parent, no positive instruction in life, no education!' Maxine said to the education authorities. 'Don has had too much of his life wasted by people who did not take the trouble to find out if he was capable of learning. Please do not keep making this mistake again and again.'

In practice, Maxine had become an advocate not only for Don, but also for all the other children given no education, because authorities deemed it unnecessary as they had severe disabilities.

'Don is participating in everyday life at home and in the community; he has developed enormously in my care. The picture you, the authorities, have of Don which has ruled his life, is wildly inaccurate! He needs to go to school now.'

Eventually there were a number of state and federal government education reviews. The 1973 Karmel report *Schools in Australia* recommended support for integration. But as the States are responsible for education, they gradually developed their policies during the following ten years, recognising that all children are entitled to an education.

The *Report of the Joint Commonwealth & State Review into the Needs of Intellectually Disabled People in Tasmania, August 1984* affirmed that all children – irrespective of their degree of disability – should be included under the provisions of the Education Act.

Maxine enrolled Don in a special school. It did not have a good outcome.

On school days Don needed a good breakfast. He was a Weetbix boy. Despite her attempts to introduce different foods, Weetbix was all he ever wanted. She crunched up the cereal, softened it with milk and began feeding him, spoonful by spoonful. He pursed his lips and turned his head away. Then back again, ready with an open mouth.

When Maxine fed Don, it was fairly quick, but she wasn't sure how much food he would have at lunchtime or how much time staff would take to feed him. Maxine named the school: 'the babysitter'. As far as she could see, that seemed to be its only role.

'I know you don't want to go, Don, but I have to go to work. We both have to do this. I have put baked beans and yoghurt in for your lunch. You choose which one you want.' Don could eye-point his preferences.

'He has to choose what he wants for lunch,' she told the teachers. 'Because he can.'

But she wasn't sure the teachers even bothered to give him a choice let alone focus intently enough to follow Don's eye pointing indications. If they were condescending, Don wouldn't cooperate, he wouldn't do it.

There were also blinks, pursed lips, groans, smiles and

screams. He made a lip sucking sound when he wanted a drink and, importantly, made an 'oh' sound for 'No'.

Don was behind in his education because he had had none, and now he was being slotted into another formal and sterile structured environment with no psychological support. *Were the poor teachers even trained properly?*

They seemed to have no idea how to relate to kids with severe disabilities. Maybe they had never had to; children like Don were still locked away in institutions, behind closed doors.

Don sat all day and he screamed. He tested his lungs and bellowed his pain or discomfort, frustration or unhappiness. He was removed from class and closed in a side room. The door was shut; there was no way of getting out. Don was trapped in his body, in his wheelchair and then in a room with no windows. Maxine had no idea that this was happening.

Perhaps the isolation was part of a behaviour modification program – an attempt at punishment and reward, like dog training, if you screamed you were punished. Feelings, just as happened back at Willow Court, were ignored. Don was punished for his extreme distress by being put into isolation in the name of 'timeout'. This was the treatment, rather than any support and comfort.

Maxine wondered if the staff even had training in special needs. They did not know how to meet him and engage with him. Don was trapped inside his spasming body, probably in undiagnosed pain, and unable to form clear words. His soul hadn't been nurtured; his trust in life hadn't been met. Now, his education was more about what it wasn't, what it was lacking, rather than focusing on Don's capabilities.

A cloud still hung over Don, with labels like 'blind' and

'severe retardation' that had been proved wrong and resoundingly rejected by Maxine.

At home, she wanted to explore other approaches to education and communication, to show and develop Don's capacities. Maxine began to experiment. She created simple communication aids, like photographs and symbols. From those, she prepared a photo album with various symbols, that fitted into different categories, like home and school, sleep, after school, family daycare, choices for food and drinks, games and feelings.

'Do you want to play with the cars or the soft toys? She would ask as she lay on the floor next to Don, resting on his beanbag. 'Do you want this story, or that story tonight?' Easy questions for Don to reply to with pointing or his yes or no responses.

Here was a boy who had experienced years of life, of feelings and thoughts. She hoped it wasn't insulting for him but she had to experiment and start somewhere. When she looked back at their early play and communication together, she could see herself as condescending.

~

Don spent time at the D'alton and Talire Special schools. He hated both. When he was eleven, nearly twelve years old, one of the teachers experimented with a basic computer that initially matched words and pictures with feelings and needs. He hoped that Don would learn how to use it, and that it would improve Don's self-esteem, knowledge and independence. But it failed, the technology was innovative but basic and Don rejected it. He still communicated with his facial expressions. This was frustrating for staff but there may have been good reasons underpinning his reactions.

Maxine understood that Don didn't have many positive human connections as a young child. Perhaps he wanted to hold onto those connections which had been so hard won and that came as he grew up. Maybe being confronted with screens was the opposite of that.

Later there was a group of children taken out of D'alton and integrated into a mainstream school with a teacher from D'alton, but Don was not part of that. Some still doubted he should ever have been in the special school at all, let alone a mainstream school.

Don was interested in, and loved being in, nature. However, rather than at least watching a film and learning about animals, Don was probably being asked very rudimentary questions and tested by being asked: 'Show me the red cup!' Had the teachers asked Don to identify different species if they were working on a nature project, he would have known. He could have pointed them out. Animals were part of his interests; he was engaged by them.

One of the part-time carers whom Maxine employed, at her own expense, was also a teacher who would do projects at home with Don. He might do a session of learning about sharks. Don loved it. He made a scrapbook and showed Maxine when she came home from work. This was exciting and, Maxine maintained, all the stuff he should have been doing at school. This young man was the first of the few carers who were really successful with Don and whom he liked and related to.

Maxine was quietly angry, in her understated way, about all the things that didn't happen for Don in his life and education; for the lack of capacity or interest from the people at school, in meeting Don where he was at. They showed no evidence of starting to connect with him from that place. To Maxine, it seemed simple.

She had been educating carers and workers to do that for some time. It was clear now, that her job was far from over.

Maxine often felt she was on a shopping spree, but what she was buying was community services and schools. She continued to explore various education options for Don. The new Steiner School sounded promising, but turned out to be just in the planning stages and would only start with kindergarten and Class 1.

It wasn't going to work for Don. He was too old and she had no idea how they would manage his disability?

Don was always 'too' something: too old, too disabled, too screamy, too quiet. However, many of her efforts were successful. She managed to source some special funding from the Department of Community Welfare so Don could attend a community school one day a week and do that with a carer.

Maxine was – inadvertently and, ultimately successfully – extending the idea of integration from childcare centres and family daycare, into primary schools.

Chapter 21

In 1983 Maxine worked on her own in a cold, dark, poky office in the Queen Alexandra in Battery Point, the old maternity hospital. The hospital housed non-government organisations only able to afford the cheap rent in the old wards. The gloomy linoleum corridors still housed oxygen tanks and still, at times, echoed with the labour pains of soon-to-be-mums and the cries of babies. Paul also, conveniently, had an office in the building and rented a space where he also lived for a while.

Maxine had moved in and out of employment. She wanted to spend more time with Don. But she was deeply aware that there were so many other children like Don. So, while she could create a future for him, she wanted a way to make that happen for more families. She felt that a Parent Action Group would be a way to get things happening. So, she created one.

Her friend David Bowling, the social worker who had supported her fostering process, was very encouraging of her vision to get it up and running. He agreed to be a founding member and helped with some of the bureaucratic details, the incorporation process, and the constitution. Similar groups had been established in other parts of Australia, but this was new model for Tasmania.

David was already familiar with how Maxine advocated for services for Don and knew she always did whatever she had to do. He admired her one-pointedness, her focus and steadfastness; her unwillingness to back down. He knew it took tenacity and courage to take on a monstrous system like Royal Derwent Hospital.

Maxine was a persuasive and impressive communicator. She spoke clearly on the phone; in meetings she didn't raise her voice. She did create enemies in the system because of her resolve to never compromise, but that was admirable. Failure was not an option. Creating an official entity gave them credibility. It meant more could be done for their cause and Maxine could try to attract funding. In 1983, the Action Group for Children with Disabilities was established. Advocacy was not a term used then, but it was precisely what Maxine was doing. The concept gained interest and grew in popularity; it began to feature more in public conversations. She developed the profile of advocacy in Tasmania.

When parents of children with disabilities arrived to see Maxine in her cramped office they met a slight woman, all energy and determination, standing beside a tall grey filing cabinet. They discussed their needs and hopes for their families.

She patiently and warmly explained what she was trying to do and, as they sat together in the room, on old swivel chairs by a desk, the parents found a generous and optimistic woman, full of enthusiasm. Despite the fact the high dingy window in her office, only let in a little light, parents drank in her positivity and left her office wondering how to match it.

They were, often, incredulous that she had fostered a child with a disability and been able to be so active and effective in this world of bureaucracy. They hoped her positivity would rub off on them and vowed to support the Action Group, somehow, any way they could.

'Maxine,' the voice said. 'Sorry to phone you at home. It's Heather. I do need to talk with you. Will you be in the office tomorrow?' Parents felt they could contact Maxine at home and talk with someone who shared their experiences.

'Yes, I will, but what is it?' Maxine stood in the kitchen doorway watching Don playing on the floor in his room.

'Oh, I am just spinning out here, Clare has been screaming all day?' Maxine recognised the tightness in Heather's slightly shrill voice.

'Is she in pain?' Maxine asked.

'Maybe. I've tried everything; it's so hard to know. Sometimes I feel I just can't go on! God, we need this respite service! I want to do whatever I can to help. I know it's not much but …'

The Action Group not only sought funds to provide advocacy and support but was planning to establish a respite service that could give parents a break from caring.

Maxine could imagine Clare, her wavy brown hair and thin body, arms flailing, strapped into her small wheelchair in Heather's kitchen.

'There are days when I just have to leave Don to scream for a few minutes,' Maxine said. 'I talk with him, try and find out what is wrong. I think maybe he is just frustrated, or pissed off, it's too hard, and all he can do to express that at times is to yell. He wants to let me know.'

'Yeah, how else can they tell us?'

'True. But you know, like Clare, he is mostly happy. She is loved, cared for, you do what you can. We all do.'

'Thanks Maxine, I know this is a crazy time to phone. Have to go, Joey is just home from school. He needs me too.'

'Okay. Come into the office tomorrow if you can.' Maxine put the phone back into its cradle. *God, it's hard for some families. I'm so glad I don't have a husband or other children. Impossible. No way I could do family and Don.*

Up until that time, professionals and volunteers who had been active in supporting families with disabilities were, in the main, paternalistic. The medical community, following the polio epidemic of the 1940s and 1950s, drove organisations like the Crippled Children's Association.

Their motivation was solid and unquestionable, but they took a much more institutional care approach. People with disabilities, or their parents, didn't guide those societies.

Maxine was at the forefront of challenging the old medical paradigm in Tasmania. She believed that people who were in an unpaid relationship with a person with a disability – such as parents and those taking a parental role – could be the most potent advocates for children because they were not going anywhere. They were there for life.

It helped to be living in Hobart, on the small island community. Parliament House and the administrative offices were all accessible, near Salamanca on the Hobart waterfront. You could bump into your local politician having a meeting or a coffee, or bowl of soup at the Retro Café, or chat with the Department workers at the local supermarket. Maxine made sure she had access to the decision makers.

She met with parents and David Bowling and the local officials, with the belief that whatever could be done should be done. There was no clear source of funding and there were late night meetings and attempts to find appropriate application forms. Maxine kept going with calm phone calls and often, obscure bureaucratic techniques were used to find a source of money. At long last, the Action Group received funding from the Commonwealth Government.

Over time, legislation and policies were changed. They now confirmed that an important role of the State was to support advocacy on behalf of the most vulnerable. A knotty problem was, that this advocacy created an ongoing tension for the Department as it funded groups that then challenged the Department's own policies and services. That was and still is, the world of advocacy.

~

While Maxine founded the Action Group in the 1980s, parents struggling with their children with disabilities were still often advised by doctors to place them into the care of institutions like Willow Court at Royal Derwent Hospital. Children like Don had poor prognoses, and the parents grappling to care for them were left with guilt. There were no alternatives.

Maxine knew one boy's family from a few years back when she had cared for him in the child's home, one of her many short-term private childcare positions. The parents were careworn with their young son and, out of desperation, had placed him in Willow Court. He died there. An accident. He slid out of his high-chair and strangled himself. *Oh, this is abuse!* Maxine thought. *He hasn't been watched; he hasn't been cared for properly.* There was an inquest. *How dare they allow this child to die? They are not getting away with it.*

'Do you mind if I ask questions?' Maxine asked his overwhelmed parents.

Maxine had no legal right to ask questions at the inquest but found a lawyer who did pro-bono work. He attended it with her and the family all huddled into a room with Maxine whispering and advising the lawyer on particular questions to ask about qualifications, equipment, and standards of care. In her mind the accident was a case of neglect.

Many interesting opportunities were offered to Maxine. She was busy with lobbying, conferences, speeches, and meetings but it was no easy task being a single Mum. She had to organise many child carers for Don.

As Maxine flicked through her diary, one day, to organise yet another carer for Don, she felt her rising guilt, the knot in her chest. She looked back, counting the various meetings she attended realising she was on twelve committees. *I can't do this; this is stupid, what is important here?* On impulse she gave it all up, deciding to be a full-time Mum at home for six months.

Still, while she loved having more time with Don, the advocacy work was pulling her back. There was such a need on both the home front as well as the wider society. She was continually torn. Her personal relationships – with women or men – didn't last; they weren't a priority. She was on another path.

Chapter 22

Don was nearly eleven in 1984, a pre-teen, still small. Maxine imagined a time when he would be an adult and would move out of home like all young people and, somehow, live independently.

She had to make that possible for him and couldn't wait until he was eighteen to think about it – she needed the Department to be involved. Otherwise, when he turned eighteen, they would step back from their parental responsibility and she and Don would be left to fend for themselves, like all the other families with young people with disabilities.

Around this time, Jean Vanier, a Catholic Canadian philosopher and humanitarian gave a talk in Newtown in Hobart. The room was packed; Maxine had to sit on the floor. His compassion for all humanity, but especially those forgotten people with disabilities was inspiring. Equally Maxine resonated with his respect for the ones that society discarded and hid away.

He put into words thoughts and feelings she carried, about the possibility of deep connection with others whatever their ability or disability.

Jean Vanier's vision was for people with disabilities to live in community houses together with those that assisted them. Maxine recognised what he was talking about. His words landed.

Yes, that's exactly what I want to do. How come you are doing what I want to do?

Here was the integration idea that Maxine had been pursuing in childcare and education, but he took the idea further, with both groups living together and learning from the other. She wanted something like that for Don. She read what she could about the communities.

Vanier had pioneered the L'Arche communities, but the strong Catholic influence behind the philosophy was an obstacle for her. She couldn't step into that religious world again; she had rejected it long ago; it had let her down.

Western Australia was pioneering the concept of group homes for people with disabilities, and she wanted to see for herself what they were doing there. So, she and Don went on a holiday to Perth.

Don's special collapsible wheelchair fitted into a normal seat. He used it in the car and next to Maxine on the plane. It had been an ordeal negotiating with the airline to agree to its use on the plane; Maxine dismantled more brick walls.

Don screamed from take-off at Hobart to Melbourne then again from take-off in Melbourne all the way to Perth. Nothing would settle him. The airline staff were frazzled and most passengers tried to block out the sound with their earphones. Maxine drank gin and tonic.

Once in Perth Maxine hired a car and they drove around for a few weeks sightseeing and checking out different group homes. She liked what she saw. *I could do that.* Though buoyed by the promise of ways to do independent supported living, she wasn't looking forward to the flight home. This time she gave Don a valium and the flight was a lot easier.

As they flew back into Hobart between low hills; Maxine looked out the cabin window and saw the River Derwent, the Bridge and Kunanyi/Mt Wellington with the city of Hobart nestled underneath. *This is home, how could I live anywhere else?*

It was a cool evening when they landed, and she carried Don down the steps of the plane onto the tarmac. The light filtered through dramatic clouds. It was clear and clean, even through the lingering fumes of aircraft fuel.

Back in Hobart, with Don sound asleep, Maxine poured a glass of wine and sat down on the couch. Thinking time.

She liked what she saw in Perth. *But do I want to move to Perth with Don? Not really.*

She couldn't imagine leaving Tasmania. It wasn't family and friends that held her. Hobart was her place, the mountain had witnessed it all, the cool weather, the bush walks, the island itself. *We could do it here. Yes, I will make it happen here in Hobart.*

But first she needed to find out why she had felt nauseous on the way home. The following day her pregnancy test came back positive. She was devastated; she had recently had a tubal ligation. It seemed to have failed. She needed to arrange another termination.

It had been such a battle to get approval for the operation to have her tubes tied. She was heading towards her late twenties, single. Doctors didn't want to accept her definitive assurance: no, she was not going to have children. They believed she was too young and that she might change her mind. But she knew her own mind and finally convinced them. Suing would have been a public process; she was a private young woman.

Chapter 23

After their travels to Perth Maxine and Don needed to move house yet again. They hadn't lived in their original home in Mt Stuart for long but had moved to Moonah. During that time Maxine applied for a Housing Department unit but – as she worked full-time then – it was not approved.

A neighbour in Moonah also owned a house in Chigwell, a suburb between Hobart and New Norfolk and was looking for a tenant. It was Housing Department stock that had been sold into the private market. Like much of Hobart, Chigwell clung to the hills and Kunanyi/Mt Wellington, its changing rock faces loomed behind in the southeast and the Derwent River meandered below. *Here we go again.* She had lived in so many places, like her parents, constant change, another rental was a common occurrence; moving house was no big deal.

Their new home was a high-set brick bungalow, painted white, with water glimpses, weaving roads and good ordinary folk in the suburb. It was sunny, north facing and Maxine hoped they could stay put for a while. Don was bigger now, thriving, well fed and growing. They needed an equipped bathroom, wide enough for his wheelchair, but even the most benevolent of landlords was never going to renovate a bathroom in a rental property. Disability access wasn't something that builders or architects considered in the mid-1980s.

A simple solution came to Maxine. She would buy the Chigwell house. But it wasn't – just like so many things in their lives – simple.

She sat in a small office on the vinyl seat in the bank waiting to be interviewed by a middle-aged man about her salary and circumstances. His grey suit looked crumpled and the air was stale. There were no windows, just him behind his wooden desk shuffling papers.

'Oh, you are working now but what if *it* gets sick,' the man said.

'I beg your pardon?' She pushed her chair back. 'He is my son!'

'It is not our policy to lend to single women, you need to have a stable job,' he said completely ignoring her comment.

You mean a husband? But she kept her mouth shut. *How dare you? I have been working all my life. What are you talking about? I have two jobs. How dare you judge my ability to work? How dare you judge Don?*

A bank mortgage was impossible. Banks did not lend to single women, let alone a single mother with a child with a disability.

She looked up to Kunanyi/Mt Wellington; swirls of cloud gently rose and fell, tendrils over the mountain. Hard rock underneath. An anchor. Someone told her of a law firm, Clerk Walker and Stops that lent money to single women. She phoned and arranged a meeting. Maxine sat in the modern office across from the thin young man who looked over her papers. There was a long silence.

He looked up at Maxine and smiled.

'Of course,' he said, 'we will just have to send someone out to look at the property. You know, we are finding that our single women customers are our best, because they don't default on their loans.'

Maxine became one of those 'best' customers and, occasionally, still uses this lawyer's services. Now, he is greyer and older but always asks after Don. A few years ago, he told Maxine, 'You taught me so much in that short time, I was amazed at what you were doing!'

Maxine and Don's new home, the first Maxine had ever owned, was light and busy. She arranged her hanging pot plants; Don had his own room. Now they could get into a routine and she could renovate the bathroom for wheelchair access.

She imagined a ramp being built at the back of the house, and wide sliding doors out to the backyard.

She thought about how to best arrange the rooms for Don and made sketches. She would need to have a wall removed so the spare bedroom could be used as an educational activity centre.

All that was going to cost quite a bit more and Maxine needed extra funds. What she didn't need, though, was the capacity to think creatively. She explored both State and Commonwealth options, hoping that, under various home modification schemes, they could share the cost. The extensive quote was for $7000.

'Don needs a home and a renovated bathroom and the only way to get a renovated bathroom is to buy a house.' Maxine told the Department of Community Welfare. 'I bought the house, the least you can do is pay for his bathroom.'

'We have no money.' Once more she heard the standard response. 'There is no money allocated for this.'

'Of course there isn't, it hasn't been done before. But that is not my problem. You are his legal guardian. Don needs a bathroom with wheelchair access for me to care for him properly.'

'Why should we pay you to have renovations done in a private house at great expense? Where will this expenditure end?'

Maxine imagined conversations flying around the Department. 'It would be cheaper to put the boy back into the residential facility The next thing she'll want is a jacuzzi and a colour television!'

What Maxine wanted was clearly outside the guidelines. There were caps on expenditure and it seemed like everything needed at least twenty people to approve it. This was a project for the bureaucracy's too-hard-basket. It could also look unfair for other children with disabilities living with their own families if money was found for renovations for Maxine.

'Don is a ward of the State,' Maxine reminded them. 'He was institutionalised for his first eight years. It was horrific and under your watch! This is your legal responsibility.' Maxine said again. 'Yes, Don may look fortunate to you, but actually he is not, he is only getting what he has a right to.'

There were probably many times when the Department would see her coming with her hands on her hips and they would think, 'Oh no, here she is again.'

Maxine found a way to save the Government about $4,500 by enlisting the services of a local builder to do the work for just $2,500. The Department eventually found the money.

Maxine's demands were not just beneficial for Don. Through her advocating for him, she was forcing the Department to think about what services needed to be developed, initially by Government and later by non-Government organisations and businesses.

The question to answer was: What was the appropriate level of support for a child with complex disabilities?

As social policy was explored, there was gradually an argument that deinstitutionalisation may be cheaper than care in large institutions. Government could save money by closing institutions.

Slowly the conversations turned around and Maxine was asked what Don would need over the coming decade into his teenage years. The Department could then start planning what the costs would be and how to meet those costs, rather than go through an ad-hoc approach.

Fortunately, change of direction was possible in Tasmania with its small population. A change in senior management could filter down quickly and create an environment where staff thought more about human rights and community programs than 'merely' budgets. There were other movements beginning to influence policy.

The important ideas of social justice and feminism were entering the conversation. Despite system and passive resistance there were never any significant barriers to relevant Ministers, and never any negative pushback to what Maxine achieved.

'Don is lucky, in a way.' Maxine said to the Department. He was one of the few who benefitted from being a ward of the State. Other parents used to look at Don's situation with envy.

When other parents of children with disabilities, discussed Maxine and Don's situation, many voiced their anger at her 'privilege' and said upsetting and offensive things to Maxine. Though it stung, Maxine did understand why.

Now Maxine had her home, a mortgage and a renovated bathroom for Don, she painted the kitchen cupboards bright yellow and set up a magnetic farm on the fridge.

She had fun creating a playroom for Don and filling it with his own bits and pieces. She placed sheets of chipboard against a wall and hung and velcroed his storybooks and toys onto it.

Don loved audiotapes too, especially those with readings of short stories. When she arranged his books, tapes and toys he would indicate, arm outstretched, and head indicating too and letting out a groan which book, tape or toy he wanted. His room had lots of hanging mobiles and photographs. She added 'silly stuff' like mobiles with cups and spoons. As she changed pictures and mobiles around, Don's big grin grew and he chuckled.

He sat in the small seat that Maxine had set up for him in the corner and in front of him were wooden boxes with different textured materials in them arranged on the floor. From the chair, he could dangle his feet to play in soapy water or paint or dirt. They both delighted in doing messy mucky things, playing together with cars and roads and animals. Don might lie on his tummy over his beanbag and Maxine would challenge him to find marbles or cars in the boxes of sand or grass.

'Find a car in the sand, Don.' As soon as he had, Maxine would 'drive' it and crash it into something; it was always the material for a great story she would make up. Don giggled.

Out in the back garden Maxine also created little corners where, on cold bright Hobart days, Don sat with his toys and small gardening tools and they dug and planted together.

Various therapists visited their home. The environment impressed them, when Maxine let them come in. She didn't always.

'Don, show how you choose your book ... or ... let's find the marbles in the sand.' She explained to the therapists how Don played and made choices, but they didn't believe her because Don wouldn't do it in front of them. 'Please Don,' she begged.

Don groaned and turned his head away and ignored Maxine. He was a smart kid and seemed to be indicating he wasn't 'on show'. He was really saying, 'Up yours.'

Maybe he had a hidden fear that if he proved his intelligence, something might happen to him. He might be taken back to Willow Court or somewhere else. He might get taken away from his Maxine.

On Don's thirteenth birthday Maxine gave him his own cassette player. He was thrilled. He had it by his bed so he could listen to stories or music when he went to bed. He could choose music or a story or nothing. He discovered the music of 'Enya' and adored her soothing music.

In the Chigwell years they often went out on weekend excursions. They would go bushwalking in Mt Field National Park. Or wander around the Botanical Gardens, past the rose garden and through the red brick archways. Maxine would place Don's wheelchair where he could smell a flower. Then, after some time smelling flowers and being shown the garden, they would settle down with a rug on the grass and have a picnic, Don out of his chair, stretched out.

Maxine wanted Don to explore, to have a go at rafting, fishing, and horse riding. They went to the Hobart Show and Maxine took him on 'dangerous rides' like the one with the big cylinder that went round and round after which the floor dropped out.

'Hang on tight Don,' Maxine said, as the floor dropped away. Their faces felt skew-whiff and their limbs were pinned to the wall. Don was ecstatic. He loved danger; he loved that sense of exhilaration. Maxine, terrified, held on tight. She would keep him safe.

Chapter 24

One afternoon, Maxine and Don sauntered down Carcoola Street in Chigwell. *Here I am, a Mum, a house, with a mortgage and Don has a friend.* As she pushed his wheelchair his arms flew out. There were grins and groans. Behind them there was a faint smattering of snow dusting Kunanyi/Mt Wellington, but closer to the river the sun warmed their faces. They stopped outside a house, leaning in over a fence to smell a bloom of white roses.

They had heard the school bell ring over the road a while back and the escalating sounds of happy end-of-school day children as they ran and squealed, bumped and laughed. Children were now out on the street on their bikes and in front yards, playing.

Suzie, a couple of years younger than Don lived two doors down the road. On their way home Don and Maxine dropped by. Her dumped school bag was by the front door. She ran down the passage to greet them.

'Can I come over, Don?' she draped her arms around his neck.

'Of course,' Maxine said.

Suzie slipped between Maxine and Don and they continued up the road, both awkwardly trying to push his wheelchair together.

At home, Maxine placed Don on the couch and Suzie lay next

to him, stretched out imitating, mirroring his posture. Maxine smiled and watched for a moment unobserved.

Maxine could hear Suzie chattering away to Don while she made some chocolate milk for them both. She cut up some fruit and mashed a banana for Don.

'Can we have a picnic, Maxine?'

'Sure, let's take it outside. Can you carry the rug for me?' Maxine bent down and gently lifted Don from the couch and carried him outside.

Later, the two played in Don's room with the magnetic farm set. Don lay on his beanbag arms outstretched while his friend moved the animals around. In another box were trains and cars and wooden blocks. Don's arm rested on the train.

'Okay, I'll make a bit of a track for the train. Here, you hold the train, Don.' Suzie built a line of wooden blocks on both sides on the carpeted floor. She guided Don's arm with the train down the middle of the track and the train chugged along the between the cliffs.

'Clickety clack, clickety clack.'

One day Suzie chose Don to be her 'show and tell' at school.

'She doesn't stop talking about Don,' the teacher said to Maxine as they arrived to introduce Don. The classroom felt very formal – all the children were in their blue uniforms.

'This is my friend, Don,' Suzie began as she hugged him at the front of her class. The children politely looked at Don and Suzie. 'He lives just up the road and we play together after school. Don is my special friend.'

Don's arms flung out wide again and he beamed. Both Suzie and Maxine took hold of a hand each. The children in the class looked a little confused. They didn't quite know what it was all about.

Maxine felt proud of Don and Suzie, but resentment had also somehow slipped in. The sadness, the sense that Don had missed out on so much school-life.

Suzie often arrived after school with little gifts for him, little trinkets. And on weekends she joined Maxine and Don on their outings. She and Don were like any neighbourhood friends, best friends and often quite competitive.

One day, they drove north to the Midlands and the historical village of Ross. As usual, Maxine had put the mattress in the back of the old van and loaded up with picnic goodies, yoghurts and fruit, and baked beans in a thermos.

They walked around the one street town and had their picnic down by the riverbank on the Macquarie River near the sandstone bridge built by convicts with its stone carvings.

'Not so close to the water,' Maxine called out to Suzie.

Don sat in his chair close to the edge and looked at his friend. His legs were outstretched; he chortled and poked his tongue out.

'Oh no, you don't, Don,' Maxine said. She could see that he wanted to kick his friend into the river if he could! She grinned to herself. She loved that Don wanted to be naughty.

Another day after school they played dress ups. Maxine dressed up too, wearing silly plastic spectacles. Maxine held the mirror for Don to see himself. More giggles. She took photos, later hanging them onto his storyboards.

Maxine made life fun even with the boring bits of having a home together. When she needed to vacuum the house, she managed to hold Don under his arms and together they attempted to push the vacuum cleaner around the house.

Late afternoon was quiet time. Don lay on his beanbag, often with Suzie beside him.

'Music time,' Suzie said. 'What would you like to listen to, Don?' His arm swung out and knocked one of the cassettes on the board onto the floor in front of him.

'I think that was just a spasm,' Maxine said, 'Let's see, which one Don?'

His arm brushed his favourite music tape. Suzie put it in the cassette player guiding Don's curled fingers to press the play button. They lay together as a soaring melody filled the room.

Maxine listened from the kitchen. All was calm in Don's room. The music had softened their mischievous playtime selves.

~

As a ward of the State, Don had never had regular contact with his biological parents. His birth mother moved to Western Australia for a number of years but did occasionally visit him at Willow Court when she arrived back in Tasmania. Don seemed to not recognise her on those visits.

A few years later, on his birthday, when Don attended Quindalup, the day centre, his birth mother surprised him with a visit. It was not prearranged and Don seemed shocked and distressed. It must have been difficult for his mother as well. Maxine had encouraged contact but after this, insisted that it be arranged in advance.

When Don's birth Mum was back living in Tasmania, she and his grandmother occasionally came down from the north of the island to visit, usually around the end of November, Don's birthday time. As they drank mugs of tea, his mother told Maxine, once again, his terrible birth story. Don listened in.

Don's mother had been informed that Don would never understand anything, and she had originally been discouraged from forming any emotional attachment to him. Yet, there he sat in his wheelchair, handsome, with short brown hair and big bright eyes. Despite being told he was blind it was now confirmed that Don had nearly normal eyesight.

His whole face would light up with a wide smile as he responded to Maxine, but he became upset, with tears and grimaces, with his birth mother's recount of his birth. He obviously understood what was being said. Maxine wanted him to have contact with his birth Mum but was clear, that it was not to include him hearing his birth story each year.

Maxine talked with the Department about the trauma reopened in those visits. Though the result was not what Maxine wanted, contact with Don's birth Mum stopped.

Chapter 25

Negotiating day-to-day life for Don was never simple and often left Maxine needing to ask for reimbursement for expenses. Even for something as simple as pyjamas.

'These winter PJs are just not working for you, Don. Let's try and find something better.' Maxine always chatted aloud, engaging Don. 'Maybe we need pyjamas made with stretch fabric so that it's easier to get them on when you have muscle spasms.'

Don needed several pairs because of incontinence and Maxine did not have a clothes dryer to make washing and drying easier. She found fabric from which to make the pyjamas and found a dressmaker to sew them. The were very well made lasting longer than bought ones, yet it took another letter to the Department requesting support to pay for them.

Often months went by with requests for extra funding for other essential items and educational costs. Approvals were made and her care for Don was acknowledged and supported but somehow the money wasn't forthcoming. This meant Maxine would have to follow up, yet again. She sought funding for a ramp hoist, this time from the City Lions Club so this one was not a cost for the Department.

Maxine occasionally used respite services to allow her a break from twenty-four-hours-a-day care. However, the arrangement was not working for Don. There was a particularly high turnover of staff and it meant he wasn't able to establish good relationships.

As a result, he did not feel secure without Maxine, particularly when the care offered was in an institutional-like setting. Maxine and other families had to fit into a restricted timetable to access a few days respite, rather than the days offered being tailored to meet the individual and families' needs. So, Maxine advocated for a live-in carer one weekend a month.

She also looked ahead and wanted to create a meaningful life for Don after he turned eighteen. Maxine reminded departmental workers again and again that she and they, needed to create as good a future as possible for a child. That, she said, is what a good parent does. The State needed to look at what it could invest in order to get the best outcomes for Don's future.

Some workers in the Department questioned what was reasonable and made assumptions about Maxine's motivations. Few people sat down with her to hear her story. Maxine was smart enough to know that she had to keep the bureaucrats onside, to not to burn the relationships. While they were not quick enough, in her estimation, to do what she wanted or, even, needed, she realised they didn't have the systems in place to accommodate all those things she wanted done.

Her allies in the Department recognised that Maxine was 'squeaky clean' in all her motives. She didn't want importance as an individual or any personal benefit, yet she stood out. She was clear about what was needed and firm about asking for it.

One senior worker understood and explained to others that Maxine as well as being a parent acted as an advocate for Don and the group of disadvantaged people that Don represented.

He thought that Maxine should not be criticised for the way she used a whole range of strategies to promote that advocacy. She had to do that because of the failure of the system.

Maxine's experiences were immensely helpful for policy development. In later years of her caring for Don, there was a major rethink of legislation and policy, not only in regards to children with a disability.

Social workers were also questioning why neglected children, young children not convicted of any criminal offence, ended up in correctional facilities. There were people with intellectual disabilities too, housed in prisons.

At home at Chigwell Don thrived and soon needed another bigger, more substantial wheelchair. There was nothing appropriate available in Tasmania. Their old van had been upgraded to a tiny Suzuki van that became their 'marshmallow van'.

Maxine and Don set off one morning and did the long drive, familiar to most Tasmanians, up the centre of the island on the Midland Highway, past scrubby bush, rocky hills, large farms, sheep and more sheep. They drove west towards Devonport, to the boat off the Island to the Mainland. Maxine steered the van up the ramp into the bowels of the ship.

From Melbourne they headed to Adelaide where Don was fitted for a custom-built wheelchair. A few years later they had to repeat this whole procedure again as Don continued to develop rapidly and outgrew his previous chair. There were two weeks of regular fittings and adjustments again in South Australia, still the only facility that manufactured the appropriate appliances.

The Department paid for a carer to go with them to help Maxine with the intense lifting and caring demands.

Meanwhile social workers continued to work towards change inside the Department so that other people like Maxine didn't have to go through such tortuous trials.

Chapter 26

After her trip to Perth back in late 1984, Maxine began to talk with the Action Group where she worked as the coordinator, about her ideas for group homes/hostels. The keen committee wanted to explore alternative models of care to create a home for children and young people with disabilities. They were mindful that it would not be another institution, but a home where young people could grow into their adulthood and have some say in determining their own futures.

If it happened – no, thought Maxine, *when* it happened – she hoped this could become a home for Don.

When he was a little older, maybe in his late teens and it was time for him to leave home, he could live there independently and stay there, safe and comfortable, into his future.

Maxine had already been researching the number of State wards in institutional care. There were a great number of children with severe disabilities who had been left in Royal Derwent Hospital and two other State institutions in Tasmania; left by parents who felt powerless and frightened with no community support to care for their children. Many became wards of the State, like Don; others were just left there in permanent care.

The thought of a group home became a force of its own; Maxine had unleashed something. Ideas flew about and different concepts were explored. In addition to researching various sources of government funding the idea was to seek money and support from service clubs and organisations for specific projects and items like wheelchairs and special beds.

Don continued to experience rapid growth spurts, making it increasingly difficult to lift him out of a conventional bed; he needed a hospital-like bed at home.

By then, there was some support for the model of community-based care, instead of care in large impersonal medical institutions. The Action Group researched options and discovered there was a possibility to seek Commonwealth funds for 'Demonstration Projects'. They prepared a submission for a group home.

They envisaged that half the residents would come from Willow Court and the other half from the community. The Action Group expected a 'no' from the funding body for their submission but, suddenly and with great relief, the response was 'yes'.

The Federal Government had found and allocated $180,000 to buy a suitable building for a community group home for five people under the auspices of the Action Group.

Maxine informed the Action Group they needed to move fast and use the money. While she generally liked quick decisions, this one came too soon, years before she or Don was ready, but they had to accept the funding. The responsibility was daunting, but fortunately, as always, her old friend Paul stood in the background. Maxine wrote down her ideas and gave them to Paul. He worked the figures, managed endless documents, dotted the 'i's and crossed the 't's and made structural sense of Maxine's dreams while she lobbied, led and moved onto the next thing.

They looked at various houses, a home in Glenorchy had

possibilities. It needed renovations; a purpose-built bathroom, two more bedrooms and a granny flat for the coordinator. The Housing Department bought the house, and as Maxine had already been through the process of renovating her home at Chigwell, she knew the requirements for people with disabilities. The Action group named it Sunlea, from its street address. They didn't want a patronising disability name.

Development of the group home progressed quickly but it all felt too rushed for Don. He was not quite fourteen-years old. The group home needed a coordinator and Maxine was the obvious choice. She planned to be there for three to five years, to successfully establish the home and, in time, withdraw from its management. This would be Don's long-term home, and she would live in the granny flat.

~

Maxine visited Willow Court often in the months before the establishment of the group home as she was determined to enable more young people to escape from there and live with Don in the community. The staff obviously remembered her from M ward, the Inquiry, and then the Inquest over the boy who died. Maxine seemed a bigger threat now than when she fought them to get Don out. She explained to everyone, to the Federal and State Governments, to Willow Court and anyone who would listen, that the institution was not appropriate.

Professionals and families discussed the benefits of deinstitutionalisation in America, the UK and then in Australia, filtering down to Tasmania. Maxine was consistent in speaking about it.

The staff and management at Willow Court probably realised it was inevitable, but their jobs and security were vulnerable.

Maxine though, was sure. She knew what she was doing was right. She believed she could jump over all the barriers. But at Willow Court her name was mud.

One morning she found the tyres of her van had been slashed. She would receive shrill phone calls in the middle of the night, she'd wake and pick up, but there was no one on the line.

Chapter 27

'Hi Pete,' Maxine had often said to the young man, in the years when she had visited Don at Willow Court. Quite tiny, with an open face and big dark eyes, he lay on his back on a mattress in one of the day rooms. Maxine was not sure whether Pete took in her greeting, but it didn't matter, she still made a point of acknowledging him.

She felt a connection with Pete as she did with other people with severe disabilities. There were lots of kids running around Willow Court, but Pete always lay in the same spot, like Don.

When Maxine knew that she was going to take Don out of Willow Court and not bring him back, even before any final approval of fostering, she made a point of telling Pete.

'I will come back and get you.' She didn't have a plan, other than not ever bringing Don back, but those words slipped out. And she never said anything that she didn't mean.

When Maxine was establishing the group home, Pete was one of the young people she wanted to live there. She managed to extract tiny pieces of information from the reluctant staff and gradually built a picture of him and some of the other residents. She discovered that Pete, a little older than Don, was also diagnosed with cerebral palsy, and had even less fluent communication than Don. Maxine later learnt about his fun sense of humour and love of music and sport.

The authorities wouldn't give Maxine any family names or contacts for Pete but she was assisted informally and contact was made with his family to ask if Maxine could visit. He wasn't a ward of the State, and that turned out to be a good thing.

Pete's family lived on the East Coast on a rundown property. Maxine wasn't sure how to have the conversation as the family wouldn't have had much understanding of what she was trying to do, her radical idea of alternative accommodation.

No one did really. It was clear to Maxine they didn't like where he was but that was all there was and, of course, they wanted the best for their Pete.

She spent half a day with his family, finding out about his early life and talking about the group home concept. They had to give permission for Pete to join Don and others at Sunlea.

'You seem to know what you are doing, so okay,' they said at the end of the day. *God, I hope so,* she thought.

~

One clear balmy day in the months leading up to the opening of the group home, Maxine walked from M ward over to the school where some of the lucky young people went for therapy. It had already been decided that Pete would move into Sunlea and Maxine talked with Alison Jacob about other young people who might join them.

Out of the building where they used to go for physiotherapy, a staff member in blue uniform pushed a contraption, like an old-fashioned wheelchair. It had a crude, purpose-built box frame sitting on it. Maxine saw that it held a girl with a lot of hair, her head dangled at quite an angle and her hands contorted backwards.

She wore a cotton skirt and was lying on her back, but her legs were drawn up almost to where the heels touched her, leaving her exposed. Maxine walked up to say hello to this tiny girl and discovered Rachel.

'Who is she?' Maxine later asked Alison. Maxine was disgusted with the way she was being cared for, seemingly with no respect for her dignity

Rachel was seventeen years old, a few years older than Don and had a very severe disability. She was not a ward of the State but still under the guardianship of her parents. *Aha*, Maxine thought.

Maxine shocked the staff by saying that Rachel should move out of Willow Court. 'Why don't you choose one of the more able-bodied children?' a staff member asked.

Once again, she informally found an address and obtained permission to visit the family. Rachel had a younger brother and her Dad was in the army.

It must have been really hard for Rachel's Mum. Like Don, the only place to go if the family needed more support at home to care for their child was Royal Derwent Hospital. Rachel's Dad was transferred away and often wasn't around to help. Her mother did her best caring for a child so severely disabled and then making the decision to put her away somewhere to be cared for. Rachel had also been placed in the Mothercraft Home in Newtown, before being sent to Willow Court.

When Maxine talked it through, she saw a huge relief in Rachel's Mum, and also reluctance, because Maxine was undoing a whole lot of matters they had come to terms with. It would be a huge decision to take Rachel out of her seemingly safe home – even if it was an institution – and place her in what would really be a new experimental group home with a small group of young people. Maxine recognised and appreciated that. It was going to be hard.

'All right then, if you have done that with Don, you must know what you are doing.'

Remarkably Rachel's parents, like Pete's, seemed to trust Maxine and they agreed. Maxine convinced them that Sunlea was a good idea with the proviso that if it didn't work, Rachel's place at Willow Court was still available.

They needed the fallback position.

Once it was known that Maxine was recruiting families for the group home, the staff, including the psychiatrist at Willow Court were aghast. They tried to discourage the families and Maxine.

'Why not choose residents (who in other people's eyes) were "more worthy"?' But of course, that went against Maxine's principles. It was difficult for her to explain to people why it was important to choose Rachel and Pete. Maxine thought they were on the scrap heap at Willow Court and she was going to get them out.

'They will die!' the psychiatrist said to Maxine.

'Well, they are better off dying in the community than at Willow Court.' She was, by then, completely unafraid of that man. She had already fought him about Don and won that battle despite being young; despite being a woman.

Maxine was used to ignorant statements in relation to Don, like, 'He is not intelligent and so, why are you bothering?' Now she had to listen to more of what she felt was drivel.

'What in heaven are you doing?' the authorities still asked. 'Wouldn't it be better to offer places to the less disabled? For them to learn living skills and be part of the community.'

They couldn't imagine what a group home experience could possibly offer Pete and Rachel who couldn't walk or even talk.

'Sorry,' Maxine said. 'If this person is breathing then we bother.' Maxine could be polite, and she could be blunt. 'What are you doing if you keep these people alive and don't want to give them a quality of life? How can you feel comfortable knowing that people are living in this environment, knowing that it is not okay?'

'No, it is not a good environment.' Some of those she spoke to agreed. 'You are right, it is not okay.' But there was, mostly, huge resistance and resentment towards what Maxine was trying to do.

'Well, if you don't allow this move to happen, why don't you just let them die?' She was expressing the direst consequences but, of course, that upset people.

'If we can do this for the most severely disabled then we make it easier for those with milder disabilities,' Maxine argued. 'If we can prove it works, then it would be a dream for people with less demanding care needs.'

When living in the community worked, it would erode the belief that people like Pete and Rachel – the ones labelled 'that kind' – belonged in institutions and hopefully open the doors for all Willow Court 'patients'.

Maxine's heart lived with the most disadvantaged. She learnt to prove to others she understood what she was talking about, even though sometimes she had no idea. She would even make stuff up, because she knew she was right. Maxine couldn't afford to let her doubters see any weakness or emotion. She needed to be on the ball, in charge at all times. She couldn't afford to make mistakes. Not one.

Maxine would not be stopped. She had to give a voice to those who were now voiceless. It was, she felt so deeply, something she did not have in her own childhood.

∼

As the pioneer and coordinator of Sunlea, Maxine needed to find appropriate staff. There weren't any people in the community who had done this kind of caring or work before, so she recruited individuals with enthusiasm who weren't burdened with previous experience, values and practices of institutional life. She wanted warm-hearted practical staff. She would train them.

'No, we are not going to have nurses or professional staff,' Maxine kept repeating, 'even with two more people with severe disabilities, as well as Don in the group home.'

As she would be living on the premises and be there virtually twenty-four hours a day, she was confident her personal experience and reassurance was enough; it was going to be okay. Her friend Paul remained a significant person in the background; he enabled things to happen.

Maxine and Don left their happy Chigwell home where they had lived for more than three years, moving into Sunlea, at the end of 1987, just after Don celebrated his fourteenth birthday.

Don had his own room in the share house and Maxine moved into the new Manager's flat adjacent to the home.

She sold the Chigwell home to her mother who moved in with her new partner. Sadly, he killed himself in that house. Maxine's Mum heard the shot ring out.

Chapter 28

Rachel had met Maxine a few times at Willow Court and knew they were moving to their new home, even though she had not been asked; her parents had decided. She had even met some of the new staff who had visited the wards at Willow Court. They were shocked. There had been a day out and a barbecue when those staff had tried to feed her sausages, after years of slops. That didn't go down too well.

In December 1987 she lay in the back of the white van. A few years later, despite her limited communication, Rachel's early memories of Sunlea were written down with the help of a worker, in her book, *Through The Window*.

Pete with his round happy face and ready grin lay beside her on the mattresses. He was sixteen and a charmer. There were no restraints. The van rocked around. At least they already knew Don. Next to them in the back of the van were six unlabelled plastic garbage bags of clothes that didn't even belong to them and boxes of medication.

Two boys in the community were also joining them; one lived with his family in rural Tasmania but attended a special school in Hobart; living in town so he could attend school was a priority. The other was physically more able, lived with his parents and went to a different school. Both of them planned to return to their families on weekends. In the beginning Rachel was the only girl.

That arrival day Rachel was excited as well as scared. The white van drove up the long driveway and then backed in to the front of their new brick home. The house, at the back a battle-axe block, was tucked away behind the street.

It was bright, airy and had four bedrooms and a large living room. The bathroom had been modified and two extra bedrooms had been built. The garden unit for Maxine was also new.

The nurses opened the back doors of the van and stood back. The new workers peered into the back of the van and then carried Pete and Rachel into their new home. Rachel's first impressions were of whirls of blue and green colours and light, white walls and a soft woven cream couch.

Maxine was furious when she saw the box of unlabelled meds, and the plastic bags. She rarely cried but she fought back hot angry tears, as she stood alone for a moment in one of the bedrooms.

She unpacked their clothes, the generic institutional too big, smelly clothes with holes in them. Most were later burnt in the incinerator out the back. The staff soon bought new individual clothes for the residents of Sunlea.

Then Maxine looked at the large box of medication. Again, there were no labels, no charts, and no written instructions, just a large box of pills. The medications were mostly diazepam; they were all prescribed that. Maxine believed the staff wouldn't give her or the Sunlea workers any information because they didn't want the move to be happening. She thought they were deliberately sabotaging it.

'And where's Rachel's wheelchair?' Maxine asked the nurses.

They shrugged. They didn't know anything about it. Of course, there were no wheelchairs.

Their first mealtime was not easy. New people, new food, new home, new sensations; apprehension and impressions whirled around for the staff and residents. Later, Rachel lay in her new bed, alone in her own bedroom. She could hear the soft voices of the staff, but she felt worried. She missed what she had always known, the staff in her old ward at least knew her. She did, eventually, fall asleep.

Chapter 29

Maxine had finally established Sunlea and moved in as the manager. Pete and Rachel were the first people to come out of Willow Court, apart from Don, with Maxine pioneering the newly developing concept of deinstitutionalisation, long before it became policy. Slowly, both the staff and young people found ways to communicate and all be together in the new home.

Sally was one of the new workers and she and Maxine knew each other vaguely – Hobart was a small town. They became close working together. They talked about their work at Sunlea and tried to imagine the feelings their residents had; being trapped in their bodies, consigned to a wheelchair, unable to feed themselves and unable to speak. Unable even to indicate a yes or a no if a person approached wanting to touch them. Being trapped in a wheelchair meant touch often came unbidden, arrived unasked for, a held hand, an arm stroked, and often, it was too soon for contact with that person, for a real yes, or a no.

Maxine didn't hang out with the lesbian community but women recognised each other and Maxine had always liked the look of Sal. She was about the same height as Maxine, slim with thin, short grey hair – not that looks were important.

She was older than Maxine; about fifteen years older. She was, in fact, close to Maxine's mother age, but a very different woman, a no-fuss kind of person. She wore jeans, shirts and jumpers and seemed independent and creative. That was attractive. Sal had an adult son and seemed to have her life sorted – unlike some of the women Maxine had known, wild women who stalked others.

Over the next few months Sal and Maxine became lovers. They enjoyed simple home cooked meals, explored art together, went for drives out of Hobart into the beautiful rolling hills, farmland and into the bush; they shared a love of nature. Sal had a great sense of humour and they chuckled together about nonsense.

Sal enjoyed a drink, as did Maxine, but Sal was also going through menopause and didn't seem to recognise that some of her mood swings were related to changes in her hormones.

Later, this caused some friction both at work and within their relationship.

~

The new Sunlea household had the summer to settle in before school started. Gradually the residents and staff learnt together. They found out about lifting and being lifted, about feeding, cooperating and communicating. Without wheelchairs the staff improvised and combined different arrangements of pillows on the couch or outside.

Pete had never had a wheelchair at Willow Court. His hours there were spent in a hammock, or on a mattress. Rachel's box one, inadequate as it was, had opened the doors at Willow Court to outside, for walks in the grounds sitting in the sun and excursions. She loved being outdoors. When Maxine requested it at Sunlea, it was another clear, 'No'.

Apparently, the chair was the property of the hospital she was told; it was only to be used by Rachel at Willow Court. Maxine went into battle again and finally the chair arrived at Sunlea.

Maxine later decided to order matrix wheelchairs for both Pete and Rachel. These had blocks of shapes that could be adjusted and moved around to accommodate different and growing bodies. They were expensive – over four thousand dollars each, so Maxine, again, had to find a source of funding.

Mealtimes were also a big learning for everyone. The residents enjoyed exploring new textures and flavours, but it was still difficult to make it an easy, enjoyable process.

Their bodies, disabled by cerebral palsy didn't necessarily respond to their internal commands of opening the mouth and chewing and swallowing. Muscles contracted involuntarily, they spasmed. Sometimes even if they wanted to, their mouths just did not open. And if the swallowing reflex did not work at the right moment, food was splattered out, or worse, went down the wrong way. In severe cases, this could cause pneumonia.

To the staff or visitors, it may have looked like some of the residents were being uncooperative. Don wanted only Maxine to feed him. Pete also often screamed in pain, sitting up to eat. And, at times, Rachel refused to eat and drink.

Not only were the residents tense at mealtimes, so were the workers. They were learning more each day and everyone was adjusting, discovering new things about each other and themselves.

Maxine often arrived at mealtimes from her unit next door with a bottle of wine for the staff in the hope of a more relaxed evening experience.

Maxine also had to find Pete and Rachel's personal bank

accounts books, held somewhere in the bureaucracy of Royal Derwent Hospital. But she couldn't find any trace of their money. A helpful friend within the system verified the existence of their accounts and the money was finally released.

Rachel later said her first year was terrible but, gradually, her sense of humour and astuteness surfaced. She liked the way the staff treated her, she could feel they respected her and slowly, with new experiences and freedom and acknowledgement of both her intelligence and feelings of uncertainty, the seeds of trust were planted.

Chapter 30

When Maxine and Don moved into the house at Sunlea, Don's black Labrador Clive, G Force, their white cat, and BC, their ginger cat moved with them. Clive padded around the house at night, sniffing at the garbage bins, and keeping the staff awake. He was both adored and hated by the residents and the staff and the cats. One night, Clive somehow ended up in the swimming pool out the back and had to be pulled out by the staff.

The young people were introduced to new experiences, so-called normal living routines and skills, each day. Pete's wide, cheeky grin that appeared when he was happy, charmed everyone. He had his music and loved being in water. At bath times and in the spa and the pool he laughed raucously. Maybe the water was an antidote to the pain he often experienced. But he didn't need words; he yelled his discomfort, his pain, especially at mealtimes sitting up.

His cerebral palsy left his body rigid and made it difficult for his body to bend.

There were family visits. Parents and siblings gradually become familiar with the new living arrangements in the house. Rachel's Mum and her little brother visited often and they would also, often, arrive with new clothes, knowing they would be just for Rachel, washed with care and put back in her room, with her trinkets and jewellery. Her own special things.

The Sunlea house slowly became a home. Pete and Rachel and Don were settling into Sunlea. So, too, where the two other young people who moved in. They had been living with their families.

The staff had to learn fast about the physical support needs of the residents. They also had to support a group of teenagers emotionally. One young man missed his Mum intensely; after a few months at Sunlea, he returned home. He did, though, become a regular visitor and friend.

At weekends the house was quieter than normal. Some residents visited their families. Maxine and Don were often off – on their own having picnics and taking drives in the little white Suzuki van. Don just fitted in the back in his wheelchair.

They went fishing often, on jetties and wharves on the Derwent River. They weren't always successful, but when they did come home with fish, they gave the catch to the cats.

As time wore on, Don struggled with sharing a house with the others. He was repeatedly unwell and seemed to be suffering from separation anxiety when Maxine wasn't with him. She took Don and some of the residents for a short holiday up the coast. But it was soon obvious that Don needed time just to be with 'his Maxine', not sharing her, not watching her care for others, lifting them, feeding them, chuckling with them, talking with them, doing all the things she used to do, just for him.

Pete and Rachel enjoyed the more relaxed time on weekends. They were taken for walks in wheelchairs around the local suburban streets, explored the shops, tried out different activities, and met new people; they enjoyed being part of the local community.

But they didn't really have to do anything. Often, they just lay around at home.

~

Since the time Maxine fostered Don and Sunlea was established, there were an increasing number of media reports about the conditions at Willow Court. It was acknowledged by the Department and the community that it was time to move some of the residents out into the community and to establish more group homes. A Community Integration Project (CIP) was set up to support people to learn life skills so they might become more independent.

As Sunlea needed another female, there were discussions with Sunlea and a teenage girl – who wasn't confined to a wheelchair – was chosen for the household. She began visiting Sunlea regularly, but Maxine had heard it would be Willow Court who would set the timetable for her moving into the house. Maxine wanted her to move in when she felt ready, not any other timing.

Under the CIP program, a 'social trainer' was employed who would teach the residents everyday living skills like dressing. This was something the young girl dived into and was so keen that she would often wake the others during the night so she could practice with all her new clothes.

That first year at Sunlea was an intense time for everyone. The residents were finding their way with shared living in the community. The workers were too. Their learning curve was steep. To some of the staff at Sunlea, Maxine was formidable. Typical of pioneers, she was feisty; she expected the staff to share her fierce passion and commitment. She was inspiring to some and scary to others. Some workers learnt to stand up for themselves and their colleagues.

Meanwhile, Don continued to struggle sharing his Mum.

Chapter 31

'It's not working, is it?' Maxine said. 'Don's unhappy, I have to change this.' Sal had arrived early for her shift at Sunlea and called in to see Maxine next door. Sal shared a house with a family friend, but spent a lot of time at work at Sunlea and snatched time with Maxine in the midst of their busy lives. They sat in the sun outside Maxine's small garden unit at the end of the long driveway, on the other side of the small silver birch trees.

'Well, I didn't know Don before, but you're right, he doesn't seem happy,' Sal said.

'He was great at Chigwell. But this,' she waved her arms about, 'all happened too fast for Don. He is not eating unless I feed him. You've seen this. And he is not sleeping well. He has tried, but it has been more than twelve months now since he moved in.'

'He did have you all to himself at Chigwell.' Sal said.

'Yes and no. There was family daycare and so-called school, lots of other people. There were babysitters,' Maxine said.

'Yeah, but in your home at night, it was just you and Don.'

'Yes, but I couldn't do that forever, it wouldn't be right for him or me. Sunlea was going to be Don's future, but it happened too early for him.' Maxine said

'I know,' Sal said.

'And it just hasn't worked.'

The air was cooling, but they sat on outside, a slight distance between. They could hear a shout from Don from the main house followed by a bark from Clive. Don's room was the closest to Maxine's unit. They turned and looked at each other.

'I am not going over there just yet,' said Maxine. 'Do you want anything to eat before your shift starts?'

'No, I ate earlier.'

They sat on in the darkening light. There were lights on in the living room and Pete's music wafted across. Maxine sat quietly, thinking. Don's wellbeing was important and so was the relationship with Sal. They had been together for about a year. *We need some space too, to explore this 'us' further.*

'I am seriously thinking of moving out of here, taking Don out of Sunlea and renting a place. Do you want to rent a house with Don and me?'

Sal leant down, picked up her coffee mug and had a sip.

It was getting cold. She looked over the rim of the mug.

'Well, that is a big thought,' Sal put her coffee down. 'Yeah, maybe.' She laughed. Max grinned back at her.

Sal stood up and took her cup back into the kitchen. 'I need to get over there, my shift starts soon.' Maxine sat on in the dark. She knew that in the future the residents of Sunlea needed to exist without her energy and presence. So did the model of care. Both needed to stand outside of 'Maxine' in order to survive. It might be good if she wasn't living on-site anymore, but if Don moved out with Maxine it would change Sunlea. The residents and staff would have to learn to find their own way together creating their unique home. Could they do it without her?

Later she recognised that many trailblazers couldn't let go of what they pioneered and stayed too long.

~

A few days after her and Sal's conversation, Maxine stood at the large living room window. She was looking out once more through the young silver birch trees, growing into their forms, their place outside the house, while inside, worlds were changing. Weekends away from Sunlea, and time with Don wasn't enough. If she left Sunlea it was going to be hard.

She and Rachel had become really close and she loved Pete too. Loved his mischievous grin and big heart and he and Don were especially good friends. It was going to be hard on everybody, except Don.

It was clear that Don still needed a close relationship with a parental figure, maybe especially since he hadn't had one in his early years. Many of the others in the group home were a little older and perhaps more able to step into the self-reliance and self-determination that came with maturity. Don seemed to be grieving for his life in his home with Maxine. It was clear he was not comfortable within himself and was regressing.

Maxine and he needed to find alternative accommodation and, again, needed the Department's support. She would have to compose another letter to the Department and she'd need Paul to look over it before she sent it. She could not afford to buy another house, but she could rent once more. Of course, bathrooms would be inadequate and as a tenant she would be unable to make the necessary alterations again. So, what were her options?

It took a few months of looking but, finally, Maxine found another house to rent, a place to create another home for Don and herself, and Sal too, making a family of sorts. But living with Don and Sal was a short-term solution. Sunlea had been Don's future, a home, a lifestyle, friends, and a structure that gave the people living there a say in their lives. This wasn't a place of just rhetoric. It was truly client centred. Sunlea was their home and they made decisions.

When Don lived with her again, his adult years ahead would loom large. The Department's Ward of the State responsibilities focused on childhood, not adulthood. Maxine knew about adulthood. Parents cared for their adult children with disabilities forever, at home. She didn't want that for Don and she wasn't going to get trapped in that life herself. *No way.*

Don needed his own home and an independent life; like any son or daughter it was his right. He would need somewhere to live as an adult and it wasn't going to be with Maxine and probably not a group home either. She would always be his Mum but not a live-in-forever Mum.

In February 1989, Maxine and Don moved out of Sunlea taking with them Clive and Don's two cats. They settled – with Sal – into a rented house, back in the Mt Stuart neighbourhood.

It became another home for Sunlea residents to visit. They now had more friends out in the community and Maxine's deep connection with Sunlea remained.

Maxine and Sal both continued working at Sunlea; Sal was there until she retired many years later. Maxine stayed on for a while and then left. Other staff came and went too, but some stayed for a very long time.

Rachel hadn't wanted Maxine to go. She had felt understood by Maxine and trusted her. Now she felt angry, betrayed and she missed her.

But Maxine was still intimately connected with Sunlea and she stepped in and pioneered personal advocates for Rachel and the other residents, so they had another friend and voice in the community.

One young woman helped Rachel to write down the things she wanted to do in her life so she could have more control over what happened to her.

This was the beginning of personal advocacy.

Chapter 32

With the establishment of Sunlea in 1987, the tide was turning. There were public inquiries and reports into the conditions at Willow Court dating back to the 1970s. There were rumbles about Willow Court and the Government deciding to downsize it. Large impersonal institutions were seen for what they were – what people like Maxine had been calling them for years – dumping grounds for people with disabilities and mental illness.

The residents hadn't chosen to live there; their basic human rights were restricted, and their quality of life was bleak. Abuse stories abounded including rumours of sexual abuse – staff having sex with patients, and patients with each other. Maxine heard rumours about babies born and killed, and abortions forced on young vulnerable women.

It wasn't just a horror story for the young people there. Those living there included women in their eighties who had been hospitalised in their fifties, women who experienced the intense emotions of menopause and were labelled 'mad' were still there thirty years later, incarcerated. Little children through to the elderly found themselves – at the end of the twentieth century – trapped in a barbaric institutional life.

Fortunately, deinstitutionalisation was on its way. And Maxine, the thin annoying young woman who challenged the bureaucrats, who confronted the psychiatrist at Willow Court and spoke up at inquiries suddenly became an important resource for the State Government.

She had proved that other people with disabilities from Willow Court, not just Don, could live successfully in the community in the Commonwealth-funded group home Sunlea. There was an alternative to the old institutional care concept that had gone on forever. She was tapped on the shoulder by the bureaucracy she had battled with for so long.

'Would you set up the first State-funded group home?' the Tasmanian Government asked Maxine.

Oh, so now you want to talk with me! She mumbled a 'Yes', but she knew it wasn't going to be a good experience. She was used to doing things her way. In her opinion, the State Government not only had too much control but they wanted things done really fast, rather than allowing a developmental process.

'You are doing this wrong,' she told a senior State Government official.

'I know,' he said. 'But this is the only way we can do it.'

Maxine worked to establish the group home at Rokeby, which was opened in April 1989. The Department bought a large, old family home, one of the first houses built at Droughty Point, on the eastern shore. It seemed remote. The home was bigger than Sunlea, with more residents. Somehow it ended up with a mini-institutional atmosphere. The large lounge room was designed to accommodate the needs of six people with wheelchairs and other equipment.

Then, there was a long corridor, and linoleum floors, with bedrooms and bathrooms off either side. In its early days as a group home, there were many staff changes. While the renovated house at Sunlea, in an established suburban street, was smaller, carpeted and adjusted to meet their needs, it was a different place to Rokeby. It was a home.

Rokeby did become a sister house to Sunlea and the Sunlea residents visited the young people there. The adolescents at Rokeby had, also, been living at Willow Court and they knew each other. The visits between the homes normalised and supported their new community living.

The deinstitution movement that had to happen gained momentum; the downsizing had begun. The process, that took nearly twenty years began with finding alternatives to the existing living arrangements and people were moved out into the community.

There were risks and obstacles during this time. They included the intransigence of the staff and unions and the difficulty of changing the work culture when closing an institution and relocating staff into other environments.

Some mini-institutions were created that potentially perpetuated the same culture. The risks of abuse were still there, particularly as there was less scrutiny in small group homes with only a couple of staff on at a time. In the early 1990s, Maxine became disillusioned and left everything to do with disability work for a while.

Willow Court had housed people with disabilities and mental illness for more than 170 years. It finally closed in 2000, under the watch of former Attorney General Judy Jackson and the horror stories still lingered in the atmosphere out at New Norfolk. Many red brick buildings became derelict; many had the charred remains of fires, signs on broken glass doors warned of asbestos. Signs warning: Do not enter.

Stories were told, even recordings made, of strange cries emanating from some of the old wards where also, some said, ghostly figures were seen. Inside some of the twenty-foot-high brick walls clawed window ledges could be seen below barred windows. Gradually many buildings were demolished.

M ward where Don had lived became a motel and painted a yellow brown. What might it be like to have slept there? Next to the motel was a restored building with large bay windows, where people living with Down's syndrome used to live. It became a nearly-elegant large antique shop, though cold inside. Small rooms still ran off the large, long ones. The old bathroom had the toilet doors off. A sink still remained. Did any of the antiques, like the rope design brass candlesticks and second-hand furniture, come from any of these buildings?

Behind large wire fences on the Royal Derwent Hospital site, another building became a community centre. A funky coffee shop was established with peaceful gardens. Some of the bleakness had disappeared. Yet the description and feeling 'bleak' still resounded in the atmosphere.

Chapter 33

Sunlea became a beacon for other group homes in the late 1980s and 1990s. Maxine wanted to ensure that residents had a say in how their own homes were managed. Rachel's mother was invited to join the Sunlea House committee in 1989. Rachel also attended the meetings and discovered that she liked the involvement in decision-making, even though it took a while to understand the complications of running a home and all the monies involved.

The residents had their own individual bank accounts. A shared household bank account in the name of Sunlea, the auspicing body, was opened and received Government funds from which workers were paid.

Rachel was appointed the house consumer representative in 1990 and attended a 2-day workshop to learn what being a representative entailed. It included supporting the residents' needs, their input into house decisions, and their involvement in the local community.

In those early years in Sunlea, there were some gradual staff and resident changes, and then structural changes.

The sunny self-contained unit where Maxine had lived, next door to Sunlea on the same block of land, was later used for individuals with disabilities. They needed some community support with independent living but had less care needs than those in the house.

The Action Group for Children with Disabilities being the auspice body for and overseeing Sunlea, also established a respite centre for children with disabilities in Glenorchy. They created holiday programs, undertook a study on families with children with disabilities, advocated for individual families and helped the Government to establish the Rokeby group home.

The vision of Maxine and the Action Group was that all the services would become independent when they were up and running successfully, each with their own incorporated bodies managing their own funding.

In practice, it became too much, and in the rush of community attitudes changing and their pioneering work, they were at risk of growing too many services. By 1993, The Action Group no longer managed Sunlea and a new organisation, Tagari Lia was established.

~

Maxine inspired many people. Her story emboldened others to observe circumstances and behaviours and to enact change. She still visited the Sunlea residents and, in the 1990s, became involved formally as an advocate through her work with the Tasmanian Advocacy and Information Service (TAISI). She encouraged and supported the process of the residents' forming relationships with their personal advocates.

Ten years after Pete, Rachel and Don moved into Sunlea, the residents had a party and invited Don and old staff, committee members and friends to celebrate with them.

During the planning of Sunlea some neighbours protested. As time passed, they recognised that the home and its residents had become the best neighbours.

Chapter 34

Maxine had two gears in her life. Full speed ahead, surging like a king tide, contributing to endless committees, attending meetings, changing policies, advocating for people.

And stopping to regroup, think and have time on her own before the next surge started again. What about Don's needs? What about herself? What about her relationship with Sal? Soon, though, she was back into the ferocity of her life. No gentle rhythmic tides.

Don continued to be at school part-time. Plus, he was regularly swimming in the heated therapy pool, on outings around Hobart and in the bush, fishing and taking walks by the beach.

Sal and Don's relationship deepened. They shared a love of music and sport, especially cricket, and together they teased Maxine about her hate for it, and most other sports. During the summer they watched test matches together and went to the cricket at Bellerive Oval.

In the winter, Don followed the AFL and his team the West Coast Eagles. Don liked Sal's meals and they enjoyed each other's sense of humour, their laconic Australian teasing humour. It was significant for Don to have another important close adult in his life. Often it was easier for Don and Sal when Maxine was at work as the dynamic of three shifted inexplicably into complicated.

Meanwhile Maxine had to find another way for Don to live an independent life. She talked with Don about what was normal for young people his age. It helped that Sal's adult son was off exploring independently, planning a trip to England and living with friends. Maxine also talked to Don about her needs as a Mum. Sal wasn't particularly part of these future conversations, but she was significantly present in both of their lives.

'What are your plans for this young man as he moves into adulthood?' Maxine asked workers in the Department again. They had supported the idea of Sunlea and the group home, but they had no plans further ahead when that did not work out for Don.

Faced with blank looks, she remarked, 'You mean to say for all these years Don has been doing all these things, living with me, with others out in the community and now you are saying you don't know what to do!'

It was still the Department's responsibility to ensure his transition from teenager to adult.

'Living in a group home does not work for Don. Are you going to put him back into an institution?' Of course, they did not want to do that, but there were no other options. So, once more Maxine had to create something new.

The years of advocacy and fighting the system had taken their toll. Although she was tired, Maxine somehow had to find the inner resources to go again, to be assertive, measured and articulate, to break through more brick walls.

'What do you think, Paul?' she asked over a coffee in Newtown. It was an ongoing conversation. 'I can't look after Don all his life. He hated living in a group home. He has to have his own place like any young person, move out of home and set up on his own. You did it. I did it. Don is going to do it too.'

'Yeah, okay. You're right. Let me think about it,' Paul said.

Plans started to whirl around as she walked along bush tracks, beside beaches, and as she drove around Hobart. She had to sort something out before Don turned eighteen, while he was still a ward of the State, still classified as a child, while the Department still had responsibility for him. Otherwise, he would be her responsibility alone for the rest of their lives. He needed his own package of funding and care, somehow.

'Here are my ideas,' Maxine said to the Department. 'Don needs financial support for carers so that he can live independently, like you do, like we all do. He needs his own home. You need to go off and fix it. Remember you are still his legal guardian!'

'That is not possible!' was the answer Maxine got. It was unheard of for the Department to fund an individual with a package of care, especially a Ward of the State entering adulthood.

Maxine soon recognised that negotiating an independent future for Don was going to be the hardest thing she had ever done. Despite everything she had been through to foster Don, to set up Sunlea, her biggest fight yet was just beginning.

'You would want this for your son or daughter. Come on, this is not extreme.' Bureaucrats recognised the terrier in her. If Maxine wanted something she would, eventually, get it.

At the same time, she always worked with the premise that she'd never ask for anything unreasonable.

'Don has a right to what every other child has, that is all. Yes, it might look like more, but it's not his fault that he is disabled and that in order for him to enjoy a life, he needs more support. You are his guardian. It is your responsibility, you didn't do this for his first eight years, so come on, now it is time.' She always tried to be rational.

Maxine realised she had to get the Housing Department on board as well. Independence meant carers, a house, money – lots more money – a program, some sort of legal body, an entity to carry all of that, to manage the money she had to find for Don. Her thoughts wound round and round.

Paul quietly did what he did best. He researched, considered options and principles.

'I think Don needs his own business,' Paul said when they met again.

'Yeah, great,' Maxine said. 'How do we do that? Can we just create a business?'

'We buy one. We buy a shelf company. There are heaps out there, cheap, easier option that starting from nothing.'

'Really, wow. I would never have thought of that. But yep, let's buy a company.'

'Then we change the name.' Paul said. 'Then the hard works starts – the Department.'

'Yeah, I won't let them say no.'

So, they bought a shelf company and renamed it D.G. Lewis Pty Ltd. And eventually the Housing Department agreed to purpose-build a house in Newtown for Don with disability access and fittings. Meanwhile they still negotiated with the Department to fund Don in his own home. It was a terrific battle. Maxine had to lobby the Department and the Minister relentlessly to enable it to fund Don according to his individual needs, nearly thirty years before the National Disability Insurance Scheme (NDIS) was pioneered.

The small, sunny, brick Housing Department unit built just

for Don in Harding Street Newtown had three bedrooms and an open kitchen living area. Sal and Maxine moved in as did teenage Don with his testosterone starting its slow and delayed ascent.

He was heading towards seventeen but had no words to express himself, and no freedom in his body to play footy, hang out with friends, to dance, paint or create music or write poetry, to release energy, emotions, confusions, and life questions. Don did remarkably well during this transition phase in the unit, considering he was trapped in his body. He was still living with Maxine and Sal but in his own home with the plan and the package being developed so that support workers would come in and be with him.

Sal and Maxine were doing less well. When it was just Maxine and Don together it seemed fine. And Sal and Don had fun together too, but the three of them together just didn't gel anymore. Even without much voice Don could play them off, be happy with one but not both, the normal teenage struggle around parenting styles and asserting his individuality.

Life was closing in on Maxine. By the early 1990s, she had to stop and figure some things out. With this next phase in Don's life starting to be sorted, there was relief but the dynamic between the three of them was claustrophobic. Something had to give. On a whim Maxine booked a month away in New Zealand in a campervan. Time alone.

On her return Maxine suggested Sal move out, short-term, so that Maxine could get Don settled, train his individual support workers and plan his day-to-day activities. Her idea was that she would move out soon, when Don and his workers were established in a routine and then she and Sal could get their relationship back on track.

That is what she thought she was saying to Sal anyway. Sal heard it differently. She heard, 'Go away, I need space.' She heard the end of their relationship. And that is what happened.

Sal continued to visit Don right up until she died of a progressive brain tumour many years later. Maxine didn't make Sal's funeral, she said her own goodbyes quietly, while staying alone on the northwest during a work trip. Don went to Sal's funeral with a support worker.

Chapter 35

'Ine, Ine' the words reverberated down the corridor at TAISI in Macquarie Street, Hobart where Maxine worked as a Disability Advocate.

'Ine, Ine.' Don's excited abbreviation of Maxine's name were the only words he seemed able to say. As a young adult, nineteen, nearly twenty years old, he made a loud entrance, full of energy and vibrancy. His arms waved about as a support worker manoeuvred his wheelchair into the meeting room for a board meeting of D.G. Lewis.

More than twelve months before Don reached his eighteenth birthday the Department finally agreed to fund a package of care. And now that D.G. Lewis, the unique company limited by guarantee, was established, Don had his own home and now his own business! It needed a Board of Directors. The Directors would be Don, Maxine and Paul.

The company was set up exclusively to support Don and was contracted to receive the State Government funding to provide twenty-four-hour support, seven days a week for him. This was going to set him up for the rest of his life with his own personal care package, his own personal support program. It was another first, another pioneering venture in Tasmania, long before the disability sector considered such an individual person-centred model of care.

At that time disability services were underfunded and fragmented, and people with disabilities had little or no choice about their access to and participation in the Tasmanian community. D.G. Lewis was all about choice for Don, and supporting him to live a meaningful life, ideally driven by Don, his choice of workers and daily activities and holidays, while his personal rights were advocated for and maintained.

Maxine and Paul administered the money with Don's input and the Department had no direct contact with Don. The company paid for Don's direct daily care and other disability costs, and his community activities. It employed five to six support staff.

Don received a disability support pension and paid his rent to the Housing Department. He saved up for his own holidays.

Perhaps not surprisingly, the package of care was never quite enough. For more than ten years Maxine and Paul contributed voluntary hours to make up the difference.

They rostered themselves onto shifts, often in the expensive overnight care timeslots, even during the years when Maxine had demanding CEO positions with non-government organisations.

What Maxine was doing, unwittingly, was showing the State Government that the package of care providing for Don's daily needs, plus his involvement in the community were the types of things they needed to be providing for other young people with disabilities, not just Don.

Today models of care like Don had, are finally being offered nationally through the NDIS. It is a move away from 'one model fits all' to individuals having a package of money and choice in service provision, and ideally in living arrangements to suit their particular interests and lifestyle. Advocacy is essential for this to happen, advocacy independent of services and Government, like the residents at Sunlea had years ago. The Government is finally implementing ideas that Maxine pioneered thirty years earlier on the island off Australia that is often left off the map.

Maxine believes the NDIS is not without its problems, especially for those children with profound disabilities. But it is based on attempting to meet the clients' needs, not prescribed by the disability services themselves, a huge shift that she pioneered for Don.

~

Paul woke to his phone. It was three in the morning.

'Sorry to call you but Don is screaming his head off,' one of Don's carers said.

'Yeah, I can hear him,' said Paul 'I'm on my way.' He lived up the road from Don and dragged himself out of bed, got in his car and drove through the dark, quiet streets. He parked and let himself into the unit at Harding Street. It was just one night out of many when he was phoned; in addition to the sleepovers he did a few nights a week, over a four-to-five-year period.

'Cerebral palsy is like a spring.' Paul had said to one of Don's support workers a few days earlier. 'There is a tension, seizures sometimes, and spasms often. It doesn't matter what sparks the tension off, it starts a sort of spiral and it gets tighter and tighter and tighter and Don can't control it. It seems to be a physical phenomenon driving the mental. One pulls on the other, the other responds.'

The workers could clearly see Don's discomfort, or was it pain or extreme inexplicable tension? Paul thought that Don knew it was happening; something set it off, maybe a dream.

'It's okay Don, it's just a dream. Go back to sleep now' the carer said, as Paul walked into Don's bedroom. No amount of sympathy seemed to help. Unfortunately, Don did not have access to appropriate medications. Maxine assumed local doctors knew little about managing cerebral palsy and weren't prepared to admit it or tap into other expertise interstate or overseas.

Don probably went through agony for years; a lack of proper pain control. Maybe, if he had had better medical care right from the beginning, and access to education, perhaps communication would have been easier for him. Don cried out, was restless but unable to move, trapped in the cycle. Paul sat down by Don's bed, the bedside light was on, and the doona was twisted and scrunched. He had to distract Don.

'One, two, three, four, five ...'

Gradually maybe some part of Don's brain stopped focusing on what was happening to him and started focusing on the numbers.

'... sixty-three, sixty-four, sixty-five ...'

All of sudden he was calm and Paul got up and walked out of the room. Don was fast asleep. The highest he ever reached was three hundred and something.

'How did you do that?' the carer asked as they walked into the living room. The television was on silently and a glow emanated from the fish tank.

'You can't make him more comfortable. It is about breaking the cycle, distracting that part of his mind that is driving this thing forward. Maybe it is the rhythm of simply counting.' Sometimes Paul just clapped his hands alongside Don's ears, bang, and that was enough.

But there were plenty of times when Paul walked away feeling totally useless. There was nothing he could do, to ease Don's discomfort.

Paul thought support workers either intuitively got it or didn't. It sounded simple but maybe the worker's own anxiety about Don's screaming in the night interfered with the success of using those techniques. The solution was also connected to intimacy and trust.

When we communicate with people without speech, when we really meet and feel met, there can be a profound feeling of acceptance. Paul knew this and the thing he treasured most about his relationship with Don was trust. It was unspoken, but closeness and confidence were either there or not. Some workers gained that trust; some didn't, like in any work situation. Except this involved intimate personal care, showering, toileting, and dressing.

Don was completely dependent on those support workers, paid employees of his company, D.G. Lewis. If Don didn't trust a worker, it was very difficult for him. The worker had a home to return to, another life. But this was Don's life.

During those years Maxine also slept over with Don a few nights a week and dropped in during the day when she could. If Maxine happened to arrive when Don was distressed, all Maxine had to do was walk into the room and his anguish melted away. Don's Maxine was with him.

Part Three

Generational healing

Happiness and loss

Chapter 36

One Saturday night after a bush walk and picnic with a friend, Maxine went to bed, tired. She woke frozen in the night, her pulse racing and feeling as if a weight was on her bed, behind her. She dared not move. She held her breath, listening. Then took a breath and opened her eyes. There was no one there.

Her heart rate gradually slowed. She lay still and quiet, tried to relax, but sleep defied her. She made a cup of tea and waited for the morning light. After that night, those suffocating feelings were there all the time. What was wrong with her?

Maxine's tucked away compartments of memories and feelings from childhood were leaking out from the separate boxes into each other. Maybe with Don more settled there was space in her soul for her buried experiences, thoughts and feelings to emerge.

'My uncles, Mum's younger brothers used to stay with us sometimes, when they were still teenagers,' she said. 'In my bed. There were no spare beds, and they crept in after I was asleep. I've never talked about this before.'

She had met a friend after work and they sat nursing their wines and talking about their families in a large, cavernous room, in the nearly empty pub in Davey Street. Maxine surprised herself as she opened up.

She was normally very private. Her teenage uncles played 'mothers and fathers' in those crowded beds down the Huon valley.

She remembered the fear that stalked her at school too, as she stumbled to talk but nothing came out or, if it did, her stammer brought jeers from the other kids.

Into the 1980s, let alone the 1960s, childhood sexual abuse was somehow tolerated, even in welfare organisations, not approved or legitimate but allowed, accepted. In one workplace a young woman with a mild intellectual disability had a pregnancy scare, and her brother was the probable father.

'It's normal in some families,' the manager said to a concerned worker.

In the early 1990s, it seemed that everybody was talking about sexual abuse. Young women and older were telling their stories, stories about fathers, teachers, family friends. It seemed like an epidemic and Maxine's stories seeped out too.

Some came out in therapy, other women started talking openly with each other and somehow the stories spoken out loud were now afforded legitimacy, were believed.

One woman followed another, doing the healing work, recovering their childhoods, naming the violence and their perpetrators, and writing their stories.

The feelings of suffocation got worse for Maxine. She wrote in her diary, trying to manage herself.

'Family secrets hidden behind closed doors could swallow you up, devour you and leave nothing. Spit you out, dead even.'

Floundering wasn't part of her self-image. She was strong, she battled bureaucracies and psychiatrists, she stepped through brick walls. Maxine had kept a lid on those inner compartments of childhood memories, but her strong sense of self was dissolving.

She heard about a woman, a therapist who specialised in sexual abuse. *Who on earth would want to do that?*

Despite her incredible drive to save Don and her outer pioneering triumphs it was time to explore her inner life. She realised that she had to take some time off work. She took on the overwhelming task of uncovering her pain that had been sealed in by that outer success. She had to stop and listen inwardly. Her therapist created a safe caring environment, listened intently. And held the space amongst disintegration and reintegration. Maxine had to put itself back together again.

Her diary was her safe place. Talking was harder.

'I feel like a jigsaw puzzle that was once briefly, colourfully whole, then it was bleached of its colour, it shattered apart …'

Graphic images wove in and out of Maxine's daily activities, along with body sensations, guilt and rage, depression and despair. Maxine moved around these shapes, these places and was also lured by death. It was a choice and not a choice, both.

'I know feelings won't kill me but sometimes they're like an automatic machine gun at my head – once you pull the trigger there is no stopping. These feelings are at times powerful enough to kill,' she wrote.

If she had known the raw intensity of therapy, the deep unravelling she might not have stepped into it; but she might not have survived either, except for Don. She had to keep going for Don. She would not leave him. But she wanted to get the hell out, out of everything, out of everywhere.

'Just one more day, one more set of anguished hours to bleed me dry – from too many tears. Only one, that's all it might take.'

~

Maxine didn't have much contact with her mother, Colleen, during that time, it was easier not to, too conflicted, but years later Colleen disclosed her fears for Maxine's safety, for her life. And in time Maxine also learnt more about her mother's difficult life, and the idea of generational trauma.

Maxine felt different to others around her, as a child, she somehow didn't belong. She watched adults, observed and wondered. She recognised contradictions and vulnerability and lived with a curiosity and concern that often started with the question 'Why?'

She later named her concern as social justice, a sincere concern for the welfare of others. This didn't come from her parents, but other influences.

At times she hated her family but was nice to them. She learnt not to question the behaviour towards her, of both love and violence. Maxine needed her Dad's protection, but he couldn't protect himself. She learnt to stay out of her Mum's way, to be quiet and good. But sometimes that wasn't enough. Colleen's rage would escape from deep inside her cage. Nostrils flared and spittle escaped her mouth as she screamed at the children, and their Dad.

When her mother hit her, Maxine hovered and watched from above. She needed to get out her body, out of herself. She drew on something, an unnamed something to get her through.

In her thirties, Maxine's angst about the pain in her childhood raged internally and helped her understand herself. It took huge courage to face what she called her 'yucky bits', hatred and cruelty. Maxine was ferocious, and that ferocity drove her in her fight for Don too.

Years later she thought, *poor Mum. Her behaviour wasn't her fault.* Her Mum went through her own pain and frailty. She had had her own childhood traumas.

Maxine had a conversation with one of the uncles, after her therapy. She was in a place of strength, the therapy had given her that, but still that conversation was like a piercing siren crying off in the distance. He told her some horrific stories of abuse within his own family, her Mum's family.

The intergenerational dysfunction, the abuse, was like a cancer going through families. Maxine's family stories, her family history was full of cracks and caverns filled with poverty, abuse, despair and isolation exacerbated by lack of education. It was inward turning in an unhealthy way, and mental health crises reverberated down the generations. Who knows what came first?

Some family patterns repeat from one generation to the next and some fortunately end. The family violence ended. But there was a parallel process. Pearl, Maxine's grandmother walked out and left her kids when Colleen, Maxine's Mum was a young teenager and Colleen had to leave school to look after her brothers.

Later Colleen repeated this, she walked out leaving a note that Tim, Maxine's youngest brother and still a teenager, found when he came home from school. Maxine was furious.

She felt a load of responsibility for both her Dad and Tim. Tim had become Colleen's favourite child and Maxine couldn't understand why she walked out. At the time her Dad had no idea about money and couldn't write a cheque to pay bills.

Over time Maxine's feelings softened into compassion and empathy for her family. She did talk with her mother many years later, just once. Her Mum summoned Maxine and said she was sorry. Her mother also spoke about her own relatives.

'It's okay now, Mum, it's all over, forgotten,' Maxine said.

She had moved on from her therapy years in her thirties. Those distant childhood memories had found a place in her life story, they were no longer hidden, shameful; they no longer shaped and pierced her experiences.

Later when Pearl became sick, Colleen too softened towards her own mother, of whom she had been critical. Colleen was also able to see her own mother as vulnerable.

Chapter 37

After Don was settled independently in his own Housing Department home and was more involved in community activities, Maxine floated. The mid-1990s were her moving around time. She bought a block of land down the Channel on Bruny Island, with a shed one street back from the beach, facing west on a quiet and peaceful bay. She often retreated there during her thirties especially between therapy sessions. She walked, she rested. Her shed was cosy and safe. A low double bed was up one end and the kitchen bench and a simple cooker up the other. Her blue and white pasta bowls nestled on the shelf.

Those pasta bowls moved with her, from Bruny to Albion Heights and later were safely housed in her cupboard in Richmond.

Maxine drifted, in rented units in North Hobart, a flat out the back of someone's house, and a lease for six months on the other side of the river at Primrose Sands, a steep block descending down to the shore, sleepy, welcoming.

She even bought a boatshed on the river near Cornelian Bay.

She was in love again with a charming woman and they shared delightful picnics, trips away, and intelligent conversation. She connected with Don, too.

But trust was not easy for Maxine. All too predictably,

Maxine's uncertainties about relationships were confirmed. As her lover crept out of her arms one night and drove back to her husband's bed she felt yet another betrayal. Perhaps the final straw, only another light piece of dried grass, but it was heavy.

Maxine was tired of duplicity and tired of moving around. She wanted her own piece of land, her own home; she wanted to plant a garden. She had been disintegrating and rebuilding her sense of self; a process of allowing herself to fall apart safely block by block and then reassemble herself brick by brick to step into the next phase of her life.

She liked the area just south of Hobart, with Kunanyi/Mt Wellington's strong presence. She bought her Albion Heights home, about fifteen minutes south of Hobart, up a steep hill, north facing, scrubby with acres of bush and a neat cottage built partly from convict bricks.

It looked up to the mountain. She planted her garden, collected firewood and slowly transformed her few acres of land.

Maxine still managed Don's twenty-four-hour-program, trained and supervised new staff, sacked other staff, and drove into town to Don's unit to sleep over a couple of nights a week. But she had found a sense of home, finally, at forty.

Even when settled into her new home Maxine's life still wasn't quite her own. Program expenses had risen, she was still juggling Don's needs and her own, juggling her time, and her sense of self. And she felt that Don wanted to be closer to her.

Her career had progressed and she stepped into her first CEO position with a volunteer organisation. One evening, home at Albion Heights from her work in the city, a glass of wine in her hand, Maxine watched the sun slip behind the mountain. She sat on the small deck outside her bedroom, by the grevilleas she had planted. They were growing well. She was tired of the overnights, tired of managing Don's program, tired of reminding Paul to do bits of the paperwork, pay slips for the workers, and to submit reports and documents to the funding body.

Maxine hated still having to rely on Paul but it had become too hard for her to supervise the staff at a distance, and they often drove her batty. She couldn't, however, stop running Don's program because who else would run it? *God I am still doing this; Don is independent but I am managing his program.* She wondered how she hadn't gone insane or succumbed to some terrible illness.

There was a chill in the air as she sipped her wine. She wondered about the possibility of building somewhere for Don on her land. Her Albion Heights house was her permanent home now. She didn't want to be anywhere else. She could borrow more money and build an independent unit there for Don, no more night drives into town, he would be nearby, she could oversee the program better, she could see him briefly and often, she could set up an intercom system for the nights, yes it could work. *It might be best for Don. It might be best for me too.*

The decision was made quickly. Maxine added more money to her mortgage, easy now she was a CEO and started the process again, with planning authorities, architects, and builders.

Soon the studio was built. Even though Don had a team of carers, Maxine was there for him last thing at night and first thing in the morning.

Support workers arrived each day in shifts. The last worker in the day helped Don into bed at night, then locked up and left. Although Maxine was nearby, Don in his early thirties was experiencing another level of independence, on his own at night.

Maxine lay on a beanbag by the fire in her olive-green living room, her quiet time before heading off to bed. *I have put so many years of my life into this young man and I have just forked out another $100,000 to build him a home. I think I have to stop now. How much more?*

Then she walked up the gravel path past the back of her house and let herself into Don's unit.

'How is it going Don? All good?' She perched on his bed. 'Was your dinner okay? I had moussaka leftovers tonight.' Don's curled fingers touched Maxine's arm.

'I know you like moussaka. Next time, I'll bring some over.' Don grinned.

'Any plans for tomorrow? I guess the footy will be on this weekend.' Maxine leant over and kissed his forehead.

'Night then, sleep well.' She locked the door behind her and stepped back into the cold Tasmanian night. She had loaded up the fire earlier and once back inside she banked it down and turned off the lights. She checked the intercom was turned up so she could hear Don if he called out in the night. She would rug up and head out into the night if he needed her.

In the morning, she checked in with Don again to make sure the worker had arrived before she left for work. The arrangements were generally working well and workers stayed overnight if she was away.

Maxine loved living on that property but at times she felt worn out doing it all on her own; managing her large dry bush block, still managing Don's program, forever employing and training new staff and working fulltime.

Summer brought the inevitable bushfire risk; she had once nearly lost her home during scorching north wind fire days. In autumn and winter there was the endless clearing of dead trees, axes and chainsaws, chopped wood and huge supplies of firewood.

Around Hobart, Maxine often saw old lovers, boys now men, and girls she had had crushes on at school pushing prams and holding toddlers' hands, mothers, maybe now grandmothers. More lovers had come and gone during her late thirties and forties, women, companionship, love and betrayal. They didn't grow into long-term relationships. Some lovers became clingy, demanding. So, out they went. People were dispensable. She relied only on herself, bottom line. A lifetime of experience affirmed that.

Maxine was often at functions alone. As a CEO she was invited to drinks at Government House. She was sometimes seen with women although she still didn't hang out at the lesbian haunts around town. More likely she was having a professional coffee meeting, speaking at a conference or at a concert when she wasn't up on her land gardening.

Maxine's life was never defined by her sexuality. She didn't like to be defined by anyone or anything, ticked, put in a box. But others tried to label her. She liked to do the unexpected, to surprise herself. So, feeling curious, she decided to check out men again.

Chapter 38

One day Maxine and Peter met for coffee. They knew each other through their work, both CEOs of community organisations. He was tall with a solid body and thick grey hair, cheerful and friendly. Maxine was surprised by how much she liked him; they talked intimately and he made her laugh.

Maxine was in her late forties and Peter was fourteen years older, healthy and ready for something new. He had recently separated from his wife after a mostly conventional family and working life. He was charming, intelligent, a joker, an orchid man, and keen on sport and Maxine and Peter quickly slipped into being lovers.

~

Maxine arranged to meet Paul for coffee. She left her office at Volunteering Tasmania and walked into town. As always, she looked up to the mountain and saw glimpses of its towering cliff faces between office blocks.

Paul worked at the old Fullers bookshop, a Hobart literary institution, then still in Collins Street.

She walked up the stairs as Paul came out of his office to meet her at the small coffee bar that overlooked the bookshelves, displayed below. She saw his hat on his desk. Paul never went anywhere without his brown hat.

Maxine shrugged off a layer of dark clothes. Paul was always happy to see her, despite their difficulties. Some people in Hobart still weren't sure if Paul and Maxine were lovers or had been lovers. Their friendship had been full of side stories, early attraction at least for Paul, and maybe too for Maxine though she was unlikely to admit that, then housemates and later colleagues. Without Paul Maxine would have struggled to set up Don's individual program.

'How are things?' Paul asked. He was still involved with the company that managed Don's care. There were funding requirements to be met, staff to be paid, and Maxine liked to talk with him about volunteering issues and government policy. He read the papers avidly and met and talked to so many Tasmanians. He had a good head.

Over time Don and Paul's friendship had changed, with their twenty-year age gap, and different interests, Paul's work and various changes in Don's living arrangements. They had moved apart but Paul continued to support the company and Maxine.

Maxine talked about work for a while and Don's program.

Suddenly she changed tack. 'I have got a boyfriend.'

'Oh,' Paul looked thoughtful. There wasn't much that Maxine could say after all those years that would surprise him. Their solid friendship both fraught, and easy had been built over nearly thirty years.

'It's somebody you know.' He did know Peter professionally. They drank their coffees, and Maxine thought about surprising herself and her friends. But she knew that Paul was happy for her.

A short while later, Peter moved into Maxine's home. She

challenged his conservative ideas, and they loved working side-by-side in the garden, eating out, having weekends away up or down the coast, bushwalking together and going to Tasmanian Symphony Orchestra concerts.

Peter got on well with Don too. Marriage had even slipped into Maxine's mind.

~

Maxine watched other people's families spill their emotions around; they were not easily mopped up, like people who threw cigarette butts from a car window up the Midland Highway, onto thirsty dry crackly grass, no awareness, flames could erupt behind them, sparks carried on the wind.

They didn't seem to care. Maxine generally stayed away from people like that. As Peter had stepped into her life she had to navigate her way through family dynamics. It was complicated.

Maxine had learnt that in order to survive she had to cut through nonsense. One evening as she and Peter lay on beanbags in front of the wood stove in her living room, they talked about how to find their way as a couple together. He had poured them a port in fine delicate glasses.

They had finished the half bottle of white before dinner and most of the Shiraz with their lamb shanks that Maxine had slow cooked.

Maxine sipped her port. It was smooth and warm and she felt mildly numbed and sleepy.

'It's outbursts I don't like. I don't mind what your kids think about me but they need to be polite, especially in my home.' She never wanted to be volatile like her Mum, she was more like her Dad; feelings rumbled around him, he didn't fight back.

'I have worked hard to create this safe place. I fight, Peter, but not in relationships. I fight for Don. Any other fights are a waste of time.'

Peter opened the woodstove and a blast of heat escaped. He poked the embers around and added another large piece of wood, shut the door and let it flame up before dampening down the flue.

'That should still be going in the morning,' he said. Maxine stroked his arm.

'It will all work out.' Peter said softly. He swallowed the remains of his port. 'Bedtime now, come my love.'

∼

Right up until she met Peter, in her late forties, Maxine had never felt fully okay sharing her bed. With every other person, Maxine clung to the edge of the bed, no matter how big the bed was, and if touched ever so slightly in the night, she was awake, alert, still, silent.

It made her relationships difficult; the sex was fine, but being in bed with another person was not. It wasn't until she met Peter that the feeling went away. Her time with him was layered and healing. Maxine couldn't believe how easy and normal she felt.

'Could we go to bed now?' Maxine asked Peter after lunch one wintery weekend, just because she wanted to be in bed with him.

'Of course,' he laughed and they undressed and slipped into crisp sheets. They cuddled and whispered together.

'You are wonderful' he said. 'I never realised loving could be so easy.'

'And I never I felt so safe.'

Chapter 39

'You've lost weight,' Maxine said to Peter one evening as they snuggled on the small couch, watching the ABC news together. They were in Peter's room, where the television lived. Their glasses of wine sat on the small coffee table. They shared Maxine's bedroom, but Peter had his own small room, and wardrobe and bathroom, as Maxine held onto threads of her independence.

'Do you think so? Yes, my clothes do feel loser,' he said as he picked up his red wine.

'You are probably eating healthier food here with me,' Maxine said.

Peter and Maxine had settled happily into their change of lifestyle, new love, shared home, holidays, lots of gardening and healthy meals.

And Maxine still had time away by herself. She headed up to Byron Bay for a few days. She escaped there every year or two, and stayed with an old friend.

Maxine and Peter talked every day while she was away and she giggled like a teenager 'in love'. This love was different from the other loves over the years not because he was a man, it simply felt right.

'How did you go at the doctors today?' Maxine asked Peter.

Wine and evening nibbles, rice crackers and humus were in front of her while butcherbirds hovered on the north-coast deck. The high-set house was nested amongst the trees and surrounded by the lush green of the subtropics, so different from her dry Tasmanian bush.

Peter had had uncomfortable reflux symptoms, probably just heartburn. He wasn't worried, but thought he had better check it out, as those uncomfortable feelings hadn't gone away. He hadn't worried Maxine by talking about it up until now. And he hadn't been to the doctor for a while either.

'Tell me about your day first.'

'I did the lighthouse walk, lots of steps but stunning views, and I saw pods of dolphins. Read my book, we had lunch at a café by the beach in Byron. It's been good, relaxing. Your turn now,' she said.

'Well, my day was not quite so relaxing,' he said. 'The doc asked lots of questions and wants to do an immediate colonoscopy.' Peter's GP had discovered other gastric symptoms and was concerned about the weight loss.

'Good to get it checked out, I guess. When?'

'Tomorrow.'

Peter had survived leukaemia a number of years previously and had a lifetime of survival stories, including TB as a child. Another medical procedure did not ring alarm bells. Except for Maxine's waking dream.

After the phone call ended, Maxine sat quietly. She looked over the trees and watched the parrots drinking nectar from the red bottlebrush flowers. She remembered that time she'd sat with Peter in North Hobart, having coffee together, two CEOs discussing some government policy. That was when she saw it.

Out of the blue, a waking dream, a sort of vision, prophetic. She was holding Peter in her arms and he was dying.

When Maxine had bought her home about ten years earlier, she had wanted to stay at Albion Heights permanently. Her relationship with Peter anchored that sense of permanence, and Maxine had hoped her life would be a little easier with Peter helping around the land and with the administration of Don's program. Maybe Paul would ease out of his role and Peter could be more involved. But disease, not ease, shadowed their relationship.

The colonoscopy diagnosed advanced bowel cancer and their cancer journey began. Bowel surgery, treatment. But it had spread.

~

Maxine and Peter's friends and families mingled on the sheltered back deck of their home at Albion Heights, away from the watchful presence of Kunanyi/Mt Wellington. A fire burned in a pot on the terrace, the barbecue was fired up and nibbles and drinks were spread out on the large outdoor table. It was the night before their April wedding. Most of the guests were aware of Peter's serious illness.

Running alongside the back of the house was the gravel pathway and gate opening onto the circular driveway up to the studio where Don lived. Don arrived that evening, his chair guided by his worker behind him, across the rough pathway and into the gathering.

'Nice to see you, Don.' Maxine's father went over to Don and touched him on the shoulder. Tim, Maxine's brother, and his family welcomed Don too. Don smiled, looked around and sounds escaped. He seemed happy.

Maxine barely believed that she was getting married the following day. She had shunned marriage, had never liked her sexuality to be labelled and she thrived on change, change she was in control of. This had happened fast and felt important especially with Peter's precarious health. At least now she would have legal rights and a say in health decisions.

She wondered what Don thought. He had known Maxine's other close women friends and lovers. Whatever was in Don's mind, he seemed delighted. Perhaps he shared a sense that his Mum was happy.

The day had been busy with runs to the airport, deliveries to the wedding venue, cooking, preparations for the evening, and packing for their trip to Victoria after the ceremony. Maxine was a gracious host despite holding off a heavy cold, and beside her Peter looked thin, but radiant.

'How about all this then, Don?' Peter said as he stood next to Don near the freestanding fire pot. 'Big family day tomorrow.' Don continued to grin.

Maxine's heavy cold worsened the following day. No one would have known. She was an expert in presenting well; camouflaging her feelings.

The morning brought one of Tasmania's clear autumn days, when the sun carried a surprising intensity, a penetrating heat. On cold days it was delicious to catch a sheltered spot and bask in its warmth. But this day was hot.

Their wedding was beautifully simple, meaningful and full of hope. Family and friends gathered outside in the gardens at Runneymede House in North Hobart a National Trust Home used for functions. Some sat and others stood, partly shaded by a large tree in a semicircle around Maxine and Peter.

Maxine's family were all there, her parents, her sister and brother, their partners and children. But some of Maxine's earlier women friends had found it hard to accept that she was getting married and to a man.

Her delicate off-white skirt was laced with darker embroidered leaves and flowers. She wore a cream satin jacket and old-fashioned elegant grey heels. Peter was in a grey double-breasted suit. His hair silvery, he stood tall. They made a striking couple.

Friends and family chatted and waited. Don sat, dressed in his smart waistcoat near the front. Simple and profound words were spoken and poems recited. Maxine and Peter stood quietly, elated as they wove their hearts and lives together.

Later Peter stood with a glass of red in one hand in the formal room overlooking the gardens.

'Thanks everyone for coming and being with us today, it means so much. Unfortunately, not all of my family were able to be here, but we celebrate together.'

Peter grinned, and spoke of his love, Maxine by his side, their fingers entwined. He was flushed, slim, handsome and proud, a man who had just married his vibrant love. The guests toasted Maxine and Peter and drank to their long and happy marriage.

A few interstate visitors noticed that Peter looked well, but thinner. As the afternoon went on Peter looked more fragile. Silently some of them wondered about their next trip to Hobart and whether they would be going to a funeral.

Chapter 40

Maxine and Peter lived the following months effusively with helicopter flights over the southwest of Tasmania, weekends on Bruny Island and up north, east coast and west. They bought two of everything, kayaks, bikes, plus a camper van and a boat. Peter grew thinner. They held onto hope, but tests had revealed spots on his liver. Peter took drugs to build up the liver to enhance its growth, before surgery to chop part of it away.

God, it is cold in here, so many half-naked people all waiting in line, in bed. Maxine looked around. Peter lay on the trolley in the waiting bay, in a flimsy, pink hospital gown; his body had a bluish tinge under the thin cotton blanket. Maxine sat beside him. He was willing to give everything a go, to live longer.

Her hands held Peter's ice-cold hands between hers, and she rubbed them to keep his circulation going. She thought of Don's tiny hands too that she had warmed all those years ago.

Peter's clothes had been placed in a brown paper bag. He looked frail. It felt undignified. Maxine looked up as staff moved from one end of the room to the other, hoping for eye contact, hoping they were important, hoping that it was Peter's turn. She pulled his thin coat up over his knees. They said nothing. They were familiar with waiting.

'We are ready for you now,' a nurse said, an hour later. They hugged and kissed. Images of scalpel, liver sliced to a fragment, and open wounds flooded Maxine as her darling Peter was wheeled away. Their eyes met, terror in his, hope in hers. They saw each other twenty-four hours later, in intensive care. He survived that surgery but the cancer had also spread to his lungs.

One night at Easter time, a few months later, after four short years together and a year of marriage, Peter died at home, with Maxine by his side, holding his hand.

~

On a clear blue day, blue as only Tasmania can do, Maxine walked at Freycinet on the east coast. She stepped out on the pink granite rocks, around the headlands, up and over to Wine Glass Bay. The funeral was over; all that was left for her was to walk, one step, then another into her grief.

Then a few months later she did it again at Lord Howe Island. She travelled with a friend and their plane landed on the tiny airstrip, nestled between sand dunes and the mountain, the only flat stretch in the middle of the island.

The small community on the island make do, they simply find ways to best live together and take care of their pristine island, recycling, selling palms, and looking after the tourists.

Maxine walked and talked; she rode a bike, climbed hills, drank in the beautiful views, and let nature nourish her; she ate, drank, and strode out on her long thin legs; she felt she could walk forever. The winter gusts blew hard but they didn't worry her; instead of being blowing her apart, they seemed to blow her grief around and bits of her back into herself.

Maxine the island girl continued to explore islands, after

Lord Howe she went alone to Norfolk Island to walk her grief some more.

~

The subtle healing that came when Peter was in her life, left her again for a time, as her grief seeped its way into everyday moments. That experience of balancing on the edge of the bed and never sleeping properly returned, she was wakeful, restless. She tried to find that safe place within herself once more; she had to climb out of that well of pain all over again.

Despite her independence she was rocked by Peter's death. The tendrils reached out years later and touched, a cold touch mostly, sometimes just a brushing. It was good when the touch had a hint of warmth in it, a memory that warmed her heart rather than chilling it in grief.

She continued to hold Peter's love and it took many more than those four, short years they had together, for Maxine to integrate her time with Peter and her loss.

Chapter 41

Maxine bought a new house in 2010, one of those spontaneous decisions she was known for, following a Sunday drive and lunch in Richmond.

She liked the all-white house, modern but with a cottage entrance, merging into the small village of old homes. She created a home for herself, a home without Peter, across the river on the other side of Hobart. Soon it was flooded with colour and furniture and paintings.

Her clothes spilled out of her walk-in robe to other cupboards in other rooms alongside some of Peter's warm jackets and summer hats that she still had. She was a funky dresser, not conventional; other women tried to emulate her style but couldn't quite carry it off.

She wore layers to work. Leggings, loose pants, flowy long tops, stylish scarves, flat chunky shoes, elegant boots, and occasionally heels. Her fine light brown hair was coloured with streaks of silver and purple and cut short.

Maxine planted food and flowers and trees as soon as she moved into her new home. She layered plants in her garden with splashes of colour like she wore her clothes, like she decorated her home. Then she built low, curved brick walls out the front near the rose bushes to enclose a cottage garden, brick edges; ones to step over, not have to break down.

She planted native shrubs to attract the birds, contracted a builder to erect a pergola, so she could be undercover for rainy days, undercover too, for intense Tassie too-hot summer days. Maxine bought paintings and sculptures on a whim to complement the bold painted walls, of deep crimsons and greens. She also dug up some soil from their Albion Heights garden where she had created a small rocky native sanctuary with Peter's ashes. She transported it to her new garden.

Maxine had forgotten how to chuckle with friends, how to share the sheer pleasure of silliness. Gradually, though, the lightness that had been missing in her life returned.

Her home became a new sanctuary, a private quiet place where she had control in her domain, her garden, and her kitchen; clean with lots of appliances, all in their place. Dogs not welcome, but a warm welcome for family and friends, when invited. And she tentatively explored a new friendship, a potential relationship with a woman she had recently met.

For a while it was like her new companion was waiting in the wings. Maxine's new friend was in love with her, while Maxine shared their loving times together. It was not rich and full like her love for Peter. Her grief had tempered this relationship that came after.

Before she had moved into her new home, fortuitously the Rudd labour government's stimulus package had funded new independent living units in a cooperative housing community in Hobart, just at the right time for Don and Maxine. It meant both she and Don could move out of her Albion Heights home, after nearly ten years; she didn't want to stay there, too many memories. It was also becoming too hard to manage the acreage on her own.

People had planned and lobbied for years for the units and suddenly money was there and the houses had to be built, quickly. Like Sunlea all those years ago, when the funding was suddenly available, the money had to be spent fast.

The move from Albion Heights did make Maxine wonder again what was going to happen to her and Don in the future. He was joyously happy at times, but also sad and frustrated. She couldn't bear to see him suffer even more. *What if he had a stroke and became even more disabled or had more chronic pain?* He had suffered enough. *What if I am not around to support him?*

The previous year Maxine had started an online counselling course during a few months she had off work after Peter died, her time for reflection. She thought about how our early experiences shape our lives.

When Don was tiny, he didn't have the loving care of a Mum, he didn't have the opportunity to fully bond with anyone for years. Maxine had always known that was not okay, but did Don know that, somewhere deep in his being? He wasn't protected, there must have been abandonment issues but somehow, he seemed to manage it.

Friends and lovers of Maxine had dropped in and out of Don's life but were not consistently there. They might hope for that personal smile, recognition, and trust when they visited Don. But why should he trust the workers or her friends. Trust was a process, built slowly.

She wondered about reincarnation. The idea struck her that there must be lots of influences in our lives. Maxine didn't think life was as simple as one birth, then death, and then a new birth.

We must be more than just genetics, made up of different somethings, threads of influences.

She did believe there was a connection between her dead brother, Geoff, and Don. Sometimes she felt Geoff hovering around Don, maybe even as Don. Or maybe Geoff's wafting presence had given them both strengths to fight their battles.

Chapter 42

On an unseasonably cold day in May, Maxine drove towards Hobart. The mountain, both a welcoming and forbidding presence, hidden from view in Richmond, appeared majestically veiled in cloud. Hobart looked small, nestled underneath.

The cloud lifted and there was a dusting of snow on the soaring mountain, sunny and beautiful. A few moments later the clouds descended again. Maxine was going to see Don, in Moonah west of Hobart, in his new home. On the way she stopped at Salamanca Market and picked up the oblong pewter name plaque she had ordered for her new house in Richmond, *Edith Pearl*, both of her grandmothers' names to honour her female heritage in her new home. She was aware of a pang of sadness too; how would her own stories be passed on?

She wandered around the market, past stalls that seemed to have been there forever, organic apples, rainbow leather belts, the large crystal stall with the man in his Akubra and the Latin American musicians – all there, in the same places, each Saturday morning. She walked past familiar faces, pinched in the cold, contracted against the biting wind and sudden burst of rain, the sort of rain that heralds more snow. The clouds had settled down low hugging the invisible mountain. Wrapped in scarves and beanies, people scurried with bags and baskets as they did their weekly Saturday morning shop. The haunting sounds of the live pan flutes and the vibrant drums of Arauco Libre, mostly Chilean refugees, accompanied them.

Later Maxine drove on through Hobart to Moonah. She parked outside the new purpose-built units, built with different shades of brick around a central driveway.

This will be Don's home now for the rest of his life. She had thought this many times before, firstly at Sunlea, then his unit in Newtown, and then on her land. All those moves just like Maxine. *This really will be Don's home for the rest of his life.*

She called out as she let herself into Don's new two-bedroom light, sunny home. The front door opened into the main living room with a large west-facing window.

The red foldout couch/day bed was open but Don lay across his blue beanbag face down, in his track pants and a t-shirt, listening to a talking book. The room was warm. Maxine sat on the floor and Don lifted his head and looked up. She turned off the book.

'Any new trophies?' she asked. Don pursed his lips.

Don's carer for the day, a woman in her forties, was nearby in the kitchen. She added a 'No.' Don went bowling each week with his friend Pete who still lived in the Sunlea Group Home.

'I won't stay long, Don, as I am getting over a cold.' Maxine said. 'Did you have a massage yesterday?' She stroked Don's neck. Don was quiet and seemed relaxed, mellow. The massage therapist came each fortnight for Don and others in the units. 'He tells you to try and keep your head straight, doesn't he?' A soft sound of assent came from Don.

'Did you watch the footy last night?'

'West Coast won,' the worker said. Don grinned. 'We have a community barbecue tomorrow.'

'Great, is everyone bringing a plate?'

'We're hoping the rain holds off so we can go shopping.' Don grinned, his whole face lit up, smiling eyes and mouth for a moment.

'We'll get a cheesecake. It's nice that the local shopkeepers know Don, now,' the carer said.

Another grin.

'That's great, Don,' Maxine said.

'Don scratched his head today,' his carer said. Maxine had noticed a healing scab on his forehead.

'Carpet burn from when he slipped of his beanbag a few days ago.'

'Yes, I saw that, it might get itchy when it's healing Don.' Maxine said. 'Well, enjoy tomorrow. I have to go now.' She stroked his face. 'See you in a few days.'

~

Don's new home, established by HOPES Inc. in 2010, was part of the first cooperative housing community for adults living with an acquired brain injury and/or neurological disability. In a suburban street in Moonah, thirteen independent living units plus a community house were built. Don was lucky to be one of the early residents accepted for the supported accommodation.

HOPES itself didn't employ personal support staff directly as they believed it was important to separate housing from support services. So, the HOPES workers were not directly involved with care for Don, but they added significantly to his social life as the residents came together as a community. They enjoyed meetings, gardening, shared meals, craft activities, and neighbourhood walks.

There were other co-op residents to interact with, a diversity of interesting people, not all of whom identified as having a disability. Don made new friends with his neighbours in the other units and enjoyed his own space. He was where Maxine hoped he would be at this stage in his life.

It worked well that the service delivery to Don and his home were separate. Previously, housing arrangements, like group homes, were financed to provide accommodation and personal care and support services to the residents with disabilities, the same service, with one provider. So, if a resident was unhappy with the care/support service provided, they would have to leave the group home and live somewhere else rather than choose a different service provider.

Generally, in group homes residents were organised together according to their care needs, rather than their personal choices. In the housing cooperative, different service providers gave support to different residents.

Don continued his daily activities, including bowling, visiting his friends at Sunlea, going to the footy, cricket and basketball, movies, holidays, picnics, and outings.

He swam regularly at the nearby hydrotherapy pool, where a carer gently cradled his head as his body sprawled and relaxed supported by the warm water. He was sometimes quiet, sometimes he vocalised loudly. His face and neck were deeply tanned, his long arms trailed as his pale body surrendered to the water.

One holiday he went on a cruise to New Zealand with a couple of support workers. They sailed up the coast and saw magnificent, rugged areas of the country as well as enjoying all the on-board activities and nightlife.

Don accessed the local shops, doctors and podiatrists, and massage therapy. But still some people stared or cringed when they saw Don out in the community, reflecting society's ableism. Sometimes out loud, they even questioned the support worker who was with Don.

'How can you work with someone like that?'

Chapter 43

Don beamed and soft creases appeared around his mouth and his eyes lit up, as he arrived for lunch at Maxine's new home in Richmond. As he sat in his wheelchair and was lowered by an electronic ramp at the back of his large white van, his worker admired Maxine's front cottage garden by the driveway.

There were two steps up to the veranda out the front and another one into the house. Maxine lugged the heavy metal tray that made a ramp, while Don waited, surrounded by lush white/pink rose bushes that lined the entrance into the house.

Short dark-hair framed Don's lively face with the beginning of faint lines but his body looked younger than his years. Because he was confined to a wheelchair, Don didn't have the movement to allow him to find a fuller adult form. His legs occasionally spasmed and shot out, sometimes perhaps deliberately. His eyes spoke his intelligence and his joy of being with Maxine.

Maxine prepared one of Don's favourite meals, a vegetable casserole. They ate at the table overlooking her backyard where fruit trees lined the back fence.

There were shouts from children navigating the maze next door and wisps of conversation over the fence. The veggie garden on the other fence was flourishing with sweet corn and leafy greens, broccoli, tomatoes and more.

Maxine fed Don mouthfuls of vegetables. He opened his mouth in anticipation and concentrated to swallow. They talked about the afternoon, a planned walk down past the Georgian houses to the famous Richmond River and the well fed ducks.

Don smiled and blinked his 'Yes,' or pursed his lips or put his tongue out for a 'No', or just didn't respond. Maxine chatted on, she had long ago developed the communication art to constantly ask questions that require only yes or no answers.

'We need sun cream and hats,' Maxine said as they prepared to walk down to the Richmond River. It was a hot February Hobart day and the sun was intense. Don laughed. He knew Maxine didn't like to wear hats; they sat uncomfortably on her fine short hair. He wore a cap and Maxine succumbed to a small, lightweight bushwalking hat. She dug out the sunglasses in his bag on the back of his wheelchair. She looked at the glasses. They were broken.

'Why don't they tell me, 'she said, 'it is so frustrating.' She looked on the kitchen bench for a spare pair of hers. He laughed at that too.

They walked in the hot sun. Up the slight hill past Georgian houses and new brick homes and older timber cottages with well-tendered gardens in the side street parallel to the busy main street in Richmond. Maxine walked behind Don's electric chair adjusting the gears up the hill and moved his cap around to shade his face as they headed down to the river.

The ducks weren't interested in the offered bread. Too well fed, they lazed in the water and under the willow trees on the other bank. The river was full. Maxine sat on a wooden bench in the shade next to Don. There was a tear, just one tear. It glided silently down the side of Don's face. Maxine didn't know why.

She could never really know exactly what Don thought or felt. She wondered about creating a living will for him. But the whole topic was fraught with pitfalls and ethical dilemmas. How could she know what Don's intentions would be in any situation? *I hope he dies before I do.*

Chapter 44

The following year Maxine, now in her mid-fifties, sipped her morning cup of tea on the back veranda. Flowers and fresh herbs lingered in the air in the garden bed in front of her and to the side the lemon tree flourished. She left the roses out the front for her Dad to manage; roses were her father's domain.

He and his partner were coming for lunch. Maxine crushed fresh basil and rosemary for the lamb. She listened to the Bach violin sonatas as she washed some potatoes to bake and made a simple green salad. The celery, lettuce, cucumbers and tomatoes all came from her vegetable garden.

'Do you remember the mutton-birds you used to cook outside, Dad?' Maxine asked as they sat around the table under her pergola a few hours later. As children they went mutton birding, all with permits to bag a decent number of birds to feed the family.

'Yes, we never cooked them inside' Maxwell said. 'You would never get rid of that fat oily smell of cooked bird flesh.'

'We ate well as kids, Dad, all that local fresh produce. And now it's fashionable again. They even have rabbit on the menu up the road at the pub,' Maxine said.

Maxwell looked like a Welsh miner, short, stocky, bred of stern stuff. The conversation shifted.

'I don't know who my father was,' Maxwell said. 'They say they didn't know his name.' Griffiths, was the family name, but it was a mystery where that surname came from. Maxine had heard the stories before, but she didn't comment. He was a good talker but it was rare that he talked about his childhood.

'Mum did her best, she was a good mother to me,' he said.

But her Nan Edith, hadn't been fair; she never told Maxwell his father's name, even on her deathbed. Who was he?

After lunch, her Dad pruned the magnificent roses that embraced the path to her front door.

'It's best to snip it here,' he said as he lent into the bush. Bees buzzed around them both and butterflies fluttered by. 'Like this. You do this branch, be courageous they like being cut right back.' As he straightened up with a slight grimace, Maxine saw that he looked older, more fragile, his short frame slightly stooped.

Later, Maxine and her Dad stood outside the front door, beside the *Edith Pearl* house name plaque, looking out over the pruned roses in the front garden. Maxine felt closest to her father but it was the grandmothers and their female lineage that called to her.

'I like it, both names together,' her Dad said.

'Both grandmothers were really special for me, strong women. I think about them more and more as I get older,' Maxine said. 'It was so good to see that as they aged, they were always cuddly together and cared for one another.'

She smiled and said a silent thank you to them both, honouring her matriarchal ancestral line of determined women. She had imbibed some of their inner strength.

~

Mount St Canice of the Good Shepherd in Hobart cared for women and girls in need. Some of the buildings still stand today high on a hill like most Catholic properties in Australia. It overlooks the River Derwent.

Maxwell's Mum Edith's story was a simple one. Her family was wealthy enough but Edith was sent to Mount St. Canice for some reason. The following generations didn't know why.

Next to the home for girls was the commercial laundry, where Edith and other girls worked, another laundry like the one up at Royal Derwent Hospital at New Norfolk. There were many laundries in Australia run by various orders of Catholic Nuns, workplaces for the girls in the homes, girls supposedly in moral danger, the so-called uncontrollable ones, the unmarriageable, pregnant and 'simple-minded' young women. They were also known as reformatories or repositories for fallen females. Horrible words. The courts sent some girls; other families left their girls there.

At Mount St. Canice the laundry provided services for hospitals and other institutions. It was also known as the Magdalena laundry, or 'The Mag'. It was run by the Order of Good Shepherd Nuns.

The girls at Mt St Canice were well fed but the conditions were brutal. The windows were barred and there was barbed wire on parts of the property; the girls were, in effect, imprisoned in another grim Tasmanian institution, like those up the river where Don had lived.

The property on the high side of Sandy Bay is now called Saint Canice. The heritage buildings have been renovated and modernised for retirement living with apartments, garden units and many facilities. It now provides care at the other end of life.

The laundry building has gone after a tragic boiler explosion that killed a number of people in 1974.

In recent years part of the truth about Edith was uncovered. She was one of the pregnant young women sent there. Her child, Maxwell Griffiths, was born out of wedlock, in 1940. He was a 'bastard' child, his father unnamed, and unknown?

Edith was a fallen woman. Who was the father of baby Maxwell? Various theories have swirled around over the years, a priest, a family member or friend?

When she left Mt St Canice as a young woman, Edith somehow kept her baby with her and avoided having him taken away and incarcerated somewhere. She must have fought hard to save him. Maxine wondered about these parallels in her family history. Edith a single parent, kept her son with her despite her own institutionalisation and society's imposed shame.

Later Edith married, providing a stepfather for her son. She had no choice; she had to marry to survive, there was no supporting parents' benefit. But she hated that man. He died when Maxine was a child.

Edith went on to live and work in housekeeping and caring for others in their homes. Maxine sometimes stayed with her in other people's homes, both of them liked that.

Edith was neat, dressed well and carried the air of a 'proper lady.' She was always supportive of Maxine doing her own thing, of not being married and staying independent. As she grew older, she remained a strong and resourceful woman despite or maybe because of her time at Mt St Canice.

Edith died when Maxine was in her late thirties.

~

As a child Maxine had liked to watch Pearl, her other grandmother. Pearl sat with one leg curled up under her bottom at the kitchen table and drank sweet milky tea in one of the many rented homes down the Huon Valley. Her thick dark hair became gingery grey. But she still had her deep belly laugh. She sank into her features and looked more Indigenous as she grew older. Across the table Colleen, Pearl's daughter and Maxine's Mum, with her dark eyes, looked like a younger version of Pearl.

Pearl's chubby fingers grasped her cup of tea as she bantered with Maxwell across the table. She liked her son-in-law; their pretend arguments were their way of expressing their fondness. Only at Christmas time did she share a bottle of longneck beer with him.

Pearl was born in an old house in Harrington Street Hobart, one of a number of children. She was a good storyteller. There were tales about gathering and collecting food down the Huon Valley and of the different places they lived. Her family also moved around often.

When Maxine was in her fifties, she asked her mother Colleen about Pearl's family, having always believed she had Aboriginal ancestors. Colleen now said she thought she was Polynesian.

Unanswered questions lingered for Maxine about her family history on both sides. Understanding her grandmothers' lives seemed important for her to make more sense of her personal and professional selves as she walked into the next phase of her life. *Had her strong female ancestry helped her save Don and break the cycle of institutionalisation?*

Chapter 45

Maxine drove out of Richmond towards her mother's home; glad she had steered past that murky place in her late thirties, when she refused to have contact with her Mum. Kunanyi/Mt Wellington loomed up ahead as always, majestic, solid and unchanging yet different each time she saw it. As she headed towards the bridge the River Derwent below looked dark, shimmery.

Maxine had lived on both sides of Hobart, the river the divider; she had swung over to the eastern shore then back to the other side and lived in southern homes. Too many places, for comfort, for stability. She liked movement and change, that is, change she could control.

As a child Maxine learnt to shut down from the shouting around her, to disconnect which meant to survive. Compartmentalising her feelings became necessary in her adult years too. Over time circumstances changed, the pace of life accelerated and society moved so quickly.

It was different for the next generation, Maxine and her brother and sister were the first generation to climb up through her family's dark histories and step out of the cycle of poverty and abuse.

On a visit a few weeks earlier, Maxine's Mum said, 'I don't have to worry about any of you, it's really good.' Maxine was there helping, digging in the little garden outside her mother's small housing department flat.

'You have all done so well!'

'Yeah, we have, all of us,' Maxine smiled. Their lives and success were so far removed from their parents' lived experience.

'Mum, are you ready?' Maxine called into the narrow dark living room. She looked inside the small unit and saw photos of her nieces and nephews on the sideboard. She was still surprised to see the one of her Don there, dressed up in a waistcoat, sitting in his wheelchair, Don not being family blood.

'Coming, just getting my bag.' Colleen said and entered the hallway, where Maxine was waiting. She was in comfortable clothes, black pants and a blouse and her thick dyed-brown hair was neatly brushed and framed her round face. Despite her hard life and smoking, her skin looked younger than other women in their early seventies.

'Your garden is looking lovely,' Maxine said as they walked outside. Deep red roses bloomed in the tiny area out the front.

'Let me know if you need any more digging.'

'The roses are good this year,' Colleen said.

Maxine wished her Mum had a larger and lighter unit, but she seemed happy in her Housing Department home. Colleen helped other residents with their gardens and organised outings and events. Her neighbours, a tight-knit group of long-term tenants were her extended family. People looked to her for guidance and support while chatting and laughing together.

Later, as she relied on her neighbours more, they became her arms and legs when she wasn't able to get out and about herself.

'Out for the day?' the neighbour asked. He stood in his kilt by his front door a few feet away.

'For a drive with Maxine,' her Mum said. They walked around the central circular garden to the car park. 'Didn't want to tell him where we are going.'

Maxine chuckled, glad for the warmth of the sun on her face, glad to finally be doing this with her Mum.

They drove east along the Brooker Highway, and then up through the city and onto the Southern outlet, towards the Huon Valley. They sat companionably, in silence.

It had been a long time since either of them had seen Geoff's grave.

They turned right before the Huon River and wound along the few kilometres beside some remaining apple orchards, past the high school and out towards the small community of Ranelagh.

Maxine pointed out the old rambling house on the left that used to be a special school.

'Do you remember, Mum? Some lunchtimes at school I walked down this road and fed the 'handicapped' kids there. I loved doing that.'

They drove past large pine trees and parked on the grass next to the small white timber Church, beside a paddock with horses calmly grazing. Maxine looked towards the tall Tasmanian gums nearby and helped her Mum out of the car.

The paint was thinning on the high walls of the small Sacred Heart Church. The sign outside the sign said 1901. Maxine leaned and looked briefly through a dusty window. There were trappings of a service, cushions and bibles. She sighed.

Mass was still held there but the Church was scheduled to be pulled down and the parish hoped to rebuild. She glanced across the road at the small rural weatherboard houses, just like the ones her family had lived in.

They found Geoff's grave, a simple concrete slab and his headstone. A stone carving of a book lay on the slab, painted white pages, with simple black faded words.

In loving memory of Geoffrey Kieran Griffiths
Called to heaven 31 December 1968
Aged 7 years
Beloved son of Colleen and Max
Safe in the arms of Jesus

'Such a long time ago,' Maxine murmured. She held her black vest around herself. Colleen was silent. They bent down and pulled weeds from Geoff's grave. Colleen's knees rested on the dry ground.

Next to him was another relative's small grave and between them was another little concrete book, this one inscribed with The Lord's Prayer.

Colleen's Mum and Dad were buried nearby, close to the vacant plot booked for Colleen, for when she would be ready to lie down beside her mother and her little boy, forever seven years old. Maxine and her mother stood awhile together; softness settled over them. Maxine wandered around the other graves. She recognised clusters of local family names, families she knew as a child in the district. It was both peaceful and melancholy.

'Oh, that's my friend's Dad there,' Maxine called over. 'And the family of my first boyfriend.'

But Colleen wasn't listening. Her fingers trailed lovingly across the words on the grave. Maxine walked back over, brushed some more leaves away and gathered up the weeds. They planned to come down again soon, with black paint to go over those tender words, written into the white concrete pages.

Chapter 46

Tasmania, the island of winds and wild places exudes softness as well, with gentle east coast blue seas, and red lichen on rounded rocks. While it is an island of contradictions, there is beauty everywhere.

The relentless Roaring Forties' mad-making winds howl around and through houses on hills, rattling windows, shaking them. The winds whip up emotions leaving people shattered, a bit wild, battered. When the wind stops the quiet is delicious and Tasmanians emerge to find sunny sitting spots. The stillness brings sanity home.

In autumn Tasmanians drive up to Mt Field and the highlands to see the fagus, the native deciduous beech; its small delicate leaves turn to vivid then burnt orange, and red. In winter Maxine didn't seek to escape, but ordered loads of dry wood, then chopped and neatly stacked it. She prepared for the cold onslaught.

The Tasmanian climate is serious. It grows people with fierce convictions, like the early Green politicians – members of Parliament who later sat on the national stage. Tasmanians are loyal, they rarely sway from their stated positions; whether supporting logging and development or being defined as 'greenies'. Individuals are delineated by their politics.

Maxine was fearless, she had fought for Don's rights, stood strong and tall, like a majestic Tasmanian Blue Gum with enduring, roots spread wide and deep into the rich Tasmanian soil. The gum bark shed often, in large strips. Maxine, too, shed. Peeled off layers from herself and created and recreated herself many times.

Originally with Don's rights in mind she eloquently presented her arguments. In fact, even today, you wouldn't want to take Maxine on in a discussion that developed into a debate. Her steely gaze remains impenetrable. She understood that it would be daunting for bureaucrats to argue against a child's basic human rights to a loving home, an education and a plan for an adult future. How could they?

She always liked working alone. She did not want her unique ideas diluted, or have doubts thrown at them. She considered problems and obstacles, in the mix of her thinking about any action and held the developing big ideas, clean and strong. She scribbled notes, drew mind maps and wrote eloquent expressive poems.

At times it was difficult for Maxine to put her ideas and her vision onto paper in a formed way. She recognised she could contract others to write up her ideas. And Paul continued for many years as a sounding board, helping, too, with practicalities, like report writing, and funding applications.

As the seasons came and went Maxine moved on from disability work through various managerial positions in non-government organisations. Apart from looking after children, coordinating childcare centres, pioneering disability changes and services, she guided volunteers, then provided advocacy and assistance for the aged. Later she worked in the mental health sector with people of all ages and their carers, seeking wellbeing and mental health support.

She stepped into those CEO roles in her forties, fifties and sixties despite leaving school after Year Ten. The lack of educational opportunities that she experienced could have limited many but not Maxine. Her young attitude towards professionals, the *I'll show you, I'm as good as you. No, I'm better than you* had mellowed. She didn't need to prove anything anymore.

She has always been a big vision/ideas person, details were tedious, except in her gardens, where she planned and grew glorious, almost sacred spaces. Maxine was good at advocacy, both at the individual level and in organisations. In more than twenty years in CEO positions, with scarce world of funding for non-government organisations, she trebled some organisations' income, gave them a public profile and expanded staff, so they could impact public policy and effect change.

Maxine's memories of her adult years merged into one another. Memory was a slippery thing. Dates didn't matter, but patterns were important in making sense of her life, in seeing the threads in a rich tapestry. Events she thought were only a few years earlier, happened much earlier. Like a course she attended or the 'Human Rights Award' she was nominated for in 2003. She was a Finalist in 2000 for Tasmanian of the Year and in 2004 she received a Member of the Order of Australia (AM) for advocacy for people with disabilities.

~

Maxine and two friends sat in the noisy shed like restaurant on the banks of Cornelian Bay in Hobart.

'Congratulations on a well deserved award.' Her friend said and they raised their glasses.

As they lowered their glasses Maxine noticed a look pass

between her two friends, a familiar look. Was it envy or jealousy that passed between the two of them? She couldn't fathom why anyone would be jealous of her; her life was full of struggle.

She stared out past them to the bay beyond, sail boats bopping about, a glimpse of the Derwent Bridge, way past the famous Boatsheds.

Earlier, Don, who was dressed up in his favourite waistcoat, jeans and shiny silk shirt, sat through it all, despite looking tired. The glittery chandeliers above, the red much-vacuumed carpet, the silver platters. Every now and then his face broke into a big smile at the waitresses. The Governor had even waited until Don arrived – late, as his new support worker took him to Parliament House instead of Government House. When he did arrive, he was full of cheer, smiles and vocal.

What an afternoon. Maxine felt drained, tense and full of classy canapés, fish nibbles and meaty treats washed down with bubbles and wine. About sixty people gathered in the reception room at Government House, balancing napkins, food and drinks. Her face was flushed, but open to the wonder of just one hour.

'Maxine Muriel Griffiths – Order of Australia Medal – for advocacy for people with disabilities in Tasmania.'

Pride, apprehension, honour and profound humility flooded her heart. Her Dad and his partner, her sister and her husband and son all shared the experience. Sadly, her Mum wasn't there, and Maxine didn't know why? She hoped Colleen had a good reason to miss the occasion.

Back in the restaurant Maxine opened the white box to find a larger medal, photos of her and a booklet outlining the meaning of the Order of Australia. Smiling she offered the booklet to her friends to read in the hope they could share her pride and humility.

With a wonderful feast and more wine and a bit of sensible chatter they sat through the next hour or so.

Yawning and tummy full Maxine suggested they all go home. That night, she crawled into bed, and her AM medal sat near under the lamplight, glistening. She rolled over, switched off the lamp and promptly fell asleep.

~

Maxine drove up the Midland Highway, thinking of all the work trips she'd done, south, north and north-west. And the terrifying road trip home down the Midland Highway in 1967. Her Mum had saved their scarce dollars and planned for a precious family holiday, a rented caravan in Devonport. After the long drive up from their home on the Cygnet Road down the Huon they arrived, hot, sticky and tired but excited to claim their bunks and unpack, especially bathers and beach towels.

Maxine was ready for days of wandering alone along the sand and collecting shells. But within a few days their trusty transistor radio told them that Tassie was on fire. The Huon Valley had been hit hard, there were reports of deaths, houses lost, animals destroyed.

They piled back into their green and white holden, despite police advice to stay put. Maxwell swore as the searing heat and wind jolted the car. They drove past paddocks that were black ash. There were smouldering fences and trees.

Even burnt sheep were still standing. The traffic was bumper to bumper as they neared Hobart. Maxine slithered further down in her seat amongst the sheets and blankets. Her Mum whimpered.

The sky was black as they wound their way down through

the old Huon highway past the mountain and Maxine wondered if their house was still there. Was her Nan dead?

Years later, as she drove north on a clear warm sunny day, Maxine felt a creeping stress again. Not bushfire stress, not stress of a State on fire, but none the less, a familiar tight feeling in her chest and gut that lived enfolded within her, usually tucked away. Somehow luck had saved her Nan and home back when Maxine was nine years old.

One-hundred-and-ten fires had raged on Black Tuesday; sixty-two people died and 7,000 were left homeless.

Now despite her sense of contentment with her life and career her breath was shallow. She shivered remembering 1967 and told herself to buckle up.

Maxine prided herself on her calm, professional approach to her work, her success in managing her teams, her relationships with government agencies and the respect from her peers. She had long proved that she could handle anything! But underneath lay her nervousness as a child, and her unease at times as an adult.

And that ever-present anxiety when her phone rang, especially during tips around the state or at night? *Has something happened to Don? Is he okay?*

The north/south divide in Tasmania was well known as NGOs scrambled for scarce resources and funding. Island loyalty was strong and so too was the fierce allegiance to their own communities in Hobart, Launceston and the North-west.

In a new CEO role Maxine inherited financial and organisational difficulties, a merger and a restructure and had to make cuts to staff. She had been chosen to manage this difficult transition. But as the weeks and months went by, criticisms mounted, and staff maintained their loyalty to the previous CEO.

'We shouldn't put up with this.' 'I don't like her.' Comments circulated.

Colleagues stopped talking when she entered the room. *Did someone really say that or am I imagining things?*

They challenged Maxine's leadership and her integrity was questioned. She reeled and felt like a clear-felled forest, decimated, unsupported. Her staff were angry at cutbacks they didn't see coming. Once more she was exhausted and on her own. Maxine wasn't sure she needed the job, but they needed her skills.

One night, around that time a loud sharp noise woke her. It was shattering glass. She waited, heart pumping, adrenalin coursing, and then stepped out of bed. Among the broken glass of her front door at her feet was a rock. Maxine phoned the police. That was the beginning of more creeping anxiety. Normally we are unaware of our heart rate, the heart graciously pumps regularly. Then there are those moments, a bushwalk, climbing a hill, a quickening, a pulse in the neck, a healthy feeling, throb, exertion, fast breaths, then the land flattens out, the breath slows.

Maxine was generally confident and went wherever she wanted to go. But the slithering feelings stayed with her, when not exercising, insidious and unseen, rising, there, and finally named as anxiety. It settled into her being and with it, again a loss of sense of her strong self. Her successful CEO bubble had burst.

There didn't seem to be a pattern to the anxiety. It arrived with her morning cup of tea on her back deck, next to her prolific basil plants; during a peaceful morning ritual, a wave of anxiety arrived. Or when driving, listening to classical music, thinking maybe not thinking, and another surge, adrenalin activated.

The police had an idea about who may have thrown the rock, but there was not enough evidence to pursue it. It didn't matter. Whoever picked up the rock from their garden or hers or someone else's, it worked. She was afraid.

Chapter 47

On cold summer mornings Maxine sat quietly wrapped in her large fluffy white dressing gown nursing cups of tea on her elegant grey couch overlooking her flourishing garden. It was her precious time for sprouting ideas for more projects and reflecting on her life; her family, friends and her relationships. However, her hovering anxiety lingered, not just in relation to her work, but they were all getting older, her parents, Don, her friend Paul. Worry, her unwelcome companion, sat beside her.

She enjoyed her current relationship with a woman, but it was so different from her time with Peter. She took pleasure in companionship, gardening and meals together, walks and weekend drives but she could never imagine living with another partner. She fiercely guarded her independence, her space. She knew that relationships carried expectations and that also created more stress.

Reflecting on family too was not always peaceful. Love and family had held conflicts and contradictions.

But as the years went by Maxine enjoyed spending more time with her family.

'There is something about blood connections,' a friend said to Maxine as they had a coffee together in Newtown. Maxine recoiled. *Here we go. Is that why Mum never fully embraced Don as her grandchild? Not a biological grandchild.* It still shocked her, that friends could make these blind comments, knowing her relationship with Don. It hurt.

Maxine was also surprised that she carried regret that she would never have grandchildren. Her parents' heritage was blurry; she did not know their stories but now understood she would not have grandchildren to pass on her own stories.

'Come for brekkie on Christmas day,' Maxine asked her sister, Sherry, at the end of 2012. 'We could all be here together.' They sat outside under the pergola in Maxine's back garden at Richmond.

'It won't leave time to cook lunch for Mum, sorry,' Sherry said.

Maxine's sister always celebrated Christmas at her home with her immediate family and her mother and mother-in-law. She lived in a high-set brick house with many steps leading up to the front door. Maxine could have Christmas there. She was often invited. There were presents for Don under the tree, but it was inaccessible for him. If Don couldn't go, Maxine would not go.

Don liked being around Maxine's family but they didn't initiate time with him. Maxine was the one who organised family occasions. She chose Don long ago as her most significant family relationship.

She visited Don on Christmas morning. He went to Sunlea for Christmas lunch with his friend Pete. Maxine went home and had a quiet afternoon, precious time alone. She stepped aside from expectations, from society, from family. For some, Christmas alone is an intensely lonely time; for Maxine, it was a peaceful day.

~

Later that year Maxine turned into the shared driveway in the Moonah units and parked again beside Don's van. She glanced in the mirror. Her short wispy hair had hints of grey and subtle highlights. She smiled to herself as she recalled her bleached and coloured hair days from long ago. She stepped out of her car knocked on the front door and entered Don's home.

As usual Don lay across a beanbag on the floor. He raised his head, and shared his happy greeting groan. Maxine slipped down onto the floor.

'How has the week been, Don?' she asked. 'I have just been to the bank. I'll give your money to the worker for shopping tomorrow.'

In the past Maxine would have encouraged Don get his own money out of the bank with a support worker. But there had been discrepancies over the years. She mostly trusted all the workers, but occasionally they let her and Don down. She had let financial trust go, taking back control.

Over time Maxine's idea of independence for Don had eroded slightly. That initial fervour of thirty years earlier had naturally dissipated. The early 1990s were heady days filled with the promise of funding possibilities, of advocacy and Don's adult life stretched ahead of him, full of potential.

Don was still involved in decision-making but less than twenty years earlier. He didn't do his own banking with a support worker, but he had the final choice in staff selection and which workers went with him on a trip across to the Mainland for a holiday. At election time Don voted. A worker helped him mark the paper after discussing it with him and asking which candidate he wanted to vote for.

'Have you any plans for today?' Maxine asked. 'I'm on my way to a meeting in Newtown.' Maxine glanced out the window. 'How are the chooks going? Many eggs?' Don chortled.

'Two this morning,' the worker said. He stood in the small kitchen, behind Maxine and Don, putting away the clean breakfast dishes. 'We talked about driving down to the park by the river and maybe taking a picnic,' he said.

'That sounds lovely,' Maxine said to Don.

The support worker went down the hallway to make the beds.

A few tears trickled down Don's face; his hands unable to wipe them away.

'What's wrong, Don? Are you feeling sick?' Maxine asked.

There was no response.

'Are you upset about something that happened today or yesterday?' Maxine placed her hand on his arm. 'Was it to do with a staff member? Maybe you are cross with me? Because I have been away and you haven't seen me much in the last few weeks?' She watched Don's face. Still no response.

'I am sorry, Don. I can't work out what it is. I am so sorry you're upset.' Maxine said.

Don's usual responses, sounds, a blink, the tongue pushed out for a 'No' were not there that day. No clear yes, no clear no. Sometimes Maxine figured it out and sometimes she didn't.

As Maxine drove away that day, she worried about getting older. Don was forty years old. She worried about herself getting older too. What would happen when she was no longer around to train staff, to employ them or to sack them? When the communication was blurred with Don, when she wasn't there to say, 'What's wrong, Don?' Not there to then try and eliminate possible causes of his distress.

After her meeting she drove the narrow and hilly streets of suburban Newtown, near the old Mothercraft home, where she first met Don, when he was three years old. She wondered how it looked now. Behind fences were large established houses and flourishing gardens. She hadn't driven those streets for a long time. She wound around a few more streets, then recognised the corner block. She drove in and sat in her car on the circular driveway drinking in the old place that was Don's home and her first place of work. *His life could have been so different if he had had love and stimulation, colours and tenderness from the very beginning.*

The building looked tired. The trees had grown since she sat with little Don in her lap, watching the leaves play games of shadows and light. A man came out of the front door that led down to the narrow steps. It was now a Salvation Army Hostel for men. Maxine drove away.

~

'Do you remember the *Annie's Coming Out* story?' A woman said a few months later, at an advisory board meeting that Maxine attended in Melbourne. It was one of the many stories that inspired Maxine. Annie Macdonald had lived in a similar institution to Don, but in Victoria, where she met Rosemary Crossley. Annie was selected to participate in a communication experiment. Rosemary became her friend and advocate, and then housemate. Annie won a legal battle to leave the institution and went onto to live a full rich life.

She wrote her story, *Annie's Coming Out*, with help from Rosemary.

Maxine's story with Don was comparable to Annie's: both diagnosed with cerebral palsy and institutionalised, both confined to wheelchairs and both unable to talk. Annie went on to learn communication aids and study at university. She travelled and presented at conferences as well as enjoying her life in Melbourne. Annie died in 2010.

Maxine did not often comment when the conversations about Annie swirled about her. She listened while the woman educated a room full of people about disability. She didn't chime in with her story of saving Don. It seemed so long ago, taking people out of Willow Court, establishing group homes and settling Don's independent care package. People forgot those early struggles. It was such passionate trailblazing time. And they forgot other children, like those hundred or so kids in southern Tasmania that didn't go to school, too disabled, too hard.

Chapter 48

In 2014 Maxine and her mother sat at the corner table, embraced by white – white walls and white chairs on the painted timber floors in the renovated cottage, up the hill at the old Signal Station at Mt Nelson. They looked out onto bushland and the sweeping views across the Derwent River, to the hills and Opossum Bay on the eastern shores in one direction and down the D'Entrecastreaux Channel in the other.

The house, built in 1811, was for the signalman who reported shipping activity on the coast. The building had had many lives apart from a family home; it housed tearooms and a café and became the Signal Station Brasserie. That day, it was Colleen's 72nd birthday.

Maxine reached for her glass of water. They had ordered their meals, looked out at the views, watched the blue wrens flittering around and talked about Maxine's brother and sister and their families.

'Your Dad played around, you know,' Colleen said.

'Oh,' Maxine looked up. She remembered the arguments as a child, but not the words. She had learnt by then to switch off from the words that were spat out in her mother's rages. She didn't want to hear them.

'And I suffered from you too … as well as your Dad's behaviour,' Colleen continued.

'Yeah, sorry Mum,' Maxine said recognising that she had closed off to years of accusations of his affairs. She had always been loyal to her Dad, not hearing, not believing. She didn't really want to hear this now either but she had to listen. Her Mum was calm, matter of fact.

They paused while their lunches arrived, fresh seafood. Now more than forty years later they both acknowledged the truth of his affairs and Maxine's loyalty to her Dad and the unspoken effect on both of them. Her Dad, Maxwell was the charmer; he had always been easy company, comfortable with a story a laugh. And her young, sociable Mum had been angry and violent.

Maxine and Colleen finished their meals and slowly wandered around the grounds outside before Maxine drove her mother home. They hugged their goodbyes briefly.

'Thanks for lunch, Maxine,' her Mum said.

'I'll phone you and see you soon.' Maxine headed back across the river to Richmond, wondering. She didn't ask her father about the affairs. The health problems of her ageing parents had begun. He was too ill; it wasn't her business. She had no reason to bring all that up from the past, it wasn't her way.

~

The following year Maxine visited both her friend and her father in hospital. The extent of her Dad's cancer was finally diagnosed while her friend was recovering from straightforward surgery. She left one ward and stepped into the lift to change floors and gears, slowly absorbing the possibility that her Dad's illness was now life threatening, he was probably dying.

Maxine sat by her Dad's bed for a while, both companionably silent. There was not much to say.

'Tim will come down from Queensland soon for a visit,' Maxine tried to engage her Dad, hoping for a spark of life about her brother's visit, but the pain and drugs had taken hold.

Phew what a day. Maxine was once more in the large hospital lift, descending to the car park. She found her car keys and headed to her car, when her mobile rang. Her sister told her their Mum had been taken into emergency with breathing problems. Maxine turned around and headed back to the lifts. *Both in hospital at the same time, what is going on?*

Although there were few available beds, Colleen was kept in for a number of days. Her breathing slowly improved with more medication.

'I want to visit your father,' Colleen said to Maxine from her hospital bed. She knew he was upstairs. 'Despite everything, I still care about him, you know.'

It was a good idea, but it would have to be delicately managed. Maxine didn't want her Mum there with her Dad's long-term partner. They had never been comfortable with each other.

Colleen didn't get to see Maxwell in hospital. She wanted to, and Maxine tried to make it happen, but her Dad wasn't up for it. A few months later, he moved into a nursing home and quietly slipped away in October 2014. Maxine was fifty-seven.

Chapter 49

If I died tomorrow, what will happen to Don? The question had lived with Maxine for a long time, generally unspoken, often hidden away in her psyche. Paul would do what he could but he was tired and she thought it was time, anyway, for him to step out of D.G. Lewis.

Earlier that year Maxine and Paul had walked down Swanson Street in Melbourne one morning. She slowed her pace to match Paul's; frustrated as she liked to step out wherever she walked, whether it was the bush or city streets. She glanced to her side, trying to not be too obvious. Yes, a limp. Yes slow. *Is Paul unfit, or is he unwell?* She watched him some more as they explored various accommodation options, researching Don's next holiday, a city holiday.

Paul still administered parts of the program, the pays and government requirements, but he didn't have a current relationship with Don. He didn't visit Don. He had put in more than twenty-five years, overnights initially, then payrolls, financial reports and the rest. She and Paul were both getting older.

They could get sick and who would manage Don's program? She worried about Don's vulnerability, how he might be treated in the future, who would be responsible to organise his care. *Who would actually care?*

Maxine and Paul both recognised that they had to think

beyond their own personal capacities to manage Don's program. Their capacities were already becoming limited.

Okay, I have to get Don's program out of D.G. Lewis, we have to move it on. Don was no longer a director as Paul and Maxine had realised that being a director on the Board of a company could have left Don with legal complications. Now it was clear they needed someone else, a different structure or organisation to manage Don's care. To employ and pay workers, plan staff rosters, care for his home and his van, negotiate with the funding body, liaise with the management of his housing coop and all the myriad of household responsibilities, small bits and pieces that added up to significant administration. All of that was overseen by D.G. Lewis, basically by Maxine.

And most importantly, someone to consult with Don about his desires and preferences, his meals, his holidays, his day-to-day life. Maybe another family could join them or there might be families to share the responsibility, under D.G. Lewis or they could create another company, or another organisation?

Yet again, Maxine had to plan for some sort of transition. She didn't want to discuss it too early with him as she knew Don could worry about this complicated process. She was concerned he might not fully understand the complex details or options, and be left with his own thoughts, swirling in his mind and having no way of sharing them with anyone.

Maxine talked with Paul and started exploring alternatives. First, she asked the Department to come up with a solution. They still had a moral, as well as a funding responsibility to Don, as a ward of the State. The Department gave her a list of possible organisations; she hoped to find a like-minded business or non-government association.

She contacted Sunlea and other disability groups asking them to put in an expression of interest to manage Don's program. She was particularly interested in their values. Sunlea was Maxine's preferred option, she hoped they might be interested in expansion, to share and educate others about their innovative operation.

They respectfully declined. Their hands were full, with their own clients and home; it did not suit them to take on more clients and programs. Maxine was disillusioned by what came back from the other three organisations, she was disturbed by their responses to the questions about values and beliefs and the practices of each service model. There was a lack of willingness to explore Don's social, emotional and spiritual needs. His physical care was only a small part of his life.

It was a stop/start process, exploring options, with more departmental discussions that came to dead ends. Maxine stopped looking for a while and went on once more with her own life and continued to manage Don's program herself. But the risks associated with being, in effect, Don's sole provider lurked in her mind.

In December 2014, Maxine began working with Beni-Abbes as the Coordinator of Outreach programs. She had stepped away from her previous overwhelming and depressing position and was having time out from the responsibilities and stresses of CEO roles. Life had come full circle and here she was again, back working with people with disabilities, reflecting on her journey with Don and thinking about his future, and again inspired by Beni-Abbes.

Jean Vanier, the Canadian whose talk Maxine had attended years before, who founded L'Arche in 1964 in France, was the visionary behind the small Beni-Abbes community in Hobart. The small not-for-profit organisation had a respected reputation, managing three households that had been operating in Hobart for many years.

Beni-Abbes offered an Outreach Service for people who live independently, but who need some support. The community comprised a range of individuals, some with disabilities, friends, assistants, Board members and volunteers. It was part of the L'Arche communities around the world.

Maxine liked the social connections between those with disabilities and so-called able-bodied people involved with the intentional community. It was the fundamental principle and ensured that people with disabilities always had friendship and support from people other than paid staff. It matched those early principles at Sunlea when residents had advocates/friends in the wider community that they could turn to for support. *This might suit Don. It may open up more personal friendships for him.*

Once more she turned to Paul. They discussed the possibility of Beni-Abbes as an organisation to manage Don's program. Paul agreed the idea was good. He was happy, as long as Maxine did the work.

Chapter 50

Maxine shared her hopes and dreams for Don's future with Beni-Abbes during 2015 adding her reflections and wisdom as an ageing parent. There were lengthy conversations as she tried to look objectively at his life: who Don was, and how he may still grow and develop as an individual in his forties and beyond. Don had a home at HOPES in Moonah for as long as he wanted, and an adequate support structure of twenty-four-hour paid support staff, with a package of funding guaranteed for as long as he required it. But he had limited friends and social connections apart from Maxine, paid workers and occasional contact with Maxine's friends.

Pete from Sunlea was his oldest friend. Despite her efforts, Maxine hadn't been able to secure a sense of belonging for Don outside her circle of love and care. Support workers often promised to visit Don when they moved on to other jobs, but it rarely happened and there was never sustained contact. A paid worker was a paid worker. Maxine wanted to offer something more for Don, the potential for a richer social life.

Maxine, impatient, had to trust once again that she would make the best decision she could. She had to make this happen while she was well, in control, settled, while both she and Don were healthy, stable and as happy as they could be. Maybe she would be around in another twenty years. But just as easily there could be an accident and she could die tomorrow or she could become ill. Her father didn't reach eighty and her mother was not well.

Don wasn't so involved in the decision transitioning his care from his company to another organisation. Somehow, he had to be okay with the final decision when it was made. And like any other person, Maxine could not control how Don responded to his various life situations and experiences. She had to let go without becoming invisible and powerless.

Beni-Abbes, with its strong principles and values, were honoured that Maxine was considering their organisation, to take on Don's program.

'You will love him,' Maxine said. Don had grown into an amazing mature and resilient man. She was relieved. It felt right.

In September 2015 Maxine wrote a letter informing Don's support workers of the coming changes of governance to Don's program and presented the idea of a nine-month transition plan.

~

Meanwhile Maxine's oldest friend, Paul, became increasingly unwell. He was diagnosed with a life-threatening condition at the end of January 2016 and Maxine worried about his health, his hopes and their friendship. She was already reflecting and reevaluating her work, relationships, her home, her future and, of course, the ongoing planning for Don's future. She once more lost a sense of herself; her 'I step through brick walls' self as she headed towards sixty.

She had struggled with menopausal symptoms for years; hot

flushes and night sweats, but now, she called them her friends. She had made the right decision about Don's program but her emotions still swirled, the gradual process of letting go of controlling his program was hard. She was tense and conflicted about other people making decisions about Don's wellbeing. That was her territory.

Maxine's commitment to him and desire to get it right for him drove her on. Apart from being 'Mum', she had always recognised Don's individual life journey, connected with but separate from hers. Her role was as a facilitator; she constructed and framed circumstances for the best possible day-to-day life for him. All the while her love shone.

During the nine-month transition, Don spent time with the Beni-Abbes community, attended social and community gatherings. Maxine supported the new coordinator employed by Beni-Abbes, and gradually reduced her long-standing role as coordinator of Don's program. She discussed the changes with Don, supporting him as always, to develop his own perspective on the changes and his future.

By July 1, 2016, Don's same support workers were now employed by Beni-Abbes instead of D.G. Lewis. Maxine resumed her role simply as Don's Mum and advocate. She had done it! *I can die peacefully now.*

It was not to be that simple.

Chapter 51

Over the last stressful year Maxine had also been worn out as the journey of her Mum's ill health accelerated and quietened, then accelerated once more. Alongside this she strode into a new CEO job with another community organisation and had fractured her wrist, which was still aching.

She found herself using all the practical advocacy skills she had developed over a lifetime to support Colleen with adequate care. Maxine and her sister, Sherry, shared some of the load while family dynamics played out alongside phone calls and updates. Maxine achieved a huge amount enabling her Mum to live out her wishes to stay at home, with extra services, equipment and support twice-a-day, seven days a week. Her Mum had a great fear of going to a nursing home.

'No, I don't want that,' her Mum said as Maxine outlined various arrangements for more support at home. 'No, I am not doing that,' to a different suggestion, something she had wanted a few weeks earlier.

Colleen was tenacious, strong-willed, and entitled to simply change her mind; she knew what she wanted and didn't want; she made quick decisions, just like Maxine. Maxine had to recognise her mother, too, was both strong and stubborn.

Colleen's lungs and heart could not function anymore after years of breathlessness and infections; her body was simply tired out and her spirited, generous, funny, caring and flirtatious nature was quiet now. It was time to go. She died on 16 April 2017.

Sherry was with her for her last breaths and Maxine arrived to her hospital bedside about ten minutes later. Her Mum looked peaceful.

Later Don held Maxine's hand as she sat next to him and told him that her mother had died. A few tears escaped down his cheek as she told him of Colleen's last days and breaths. Don looked directly into Maxine's eyes as he had done forty years earlier cradled in her lap at the Mothercraft home. *What a beautiful man.* Colleen was buried in the Ranelagh Cemetery, near the grave of her little boy, Geoff.

~

A month later in May 2017, Maxine spoke on behalf of Don at his dear friend Pete's funeral. Pete had apparently died from complications from the horrible flu doing the rounds that winter. Maxine read out Don's words that she and Don had prepared together.

> "I have known Pete since we were around four or five years old. We both lived at Willow Court, in New Norfolk until I was eight and went to live with my Mum Maxine. Pete and I lived on M Ward and we spent a lot of time in the nursery section of the ward lounging around on pillows and mattresses on the floor. We didn't have much opportunity to actually play together but we kind of knew each other was around.

Our special friendship began then – just lounging around but aware of each other. After I moved out and went to live with Mum, Pete and I lost contact for a few years but we sure didn't forget each other.

When Sunlea was being set up Pete was invited to come to live there with me and a few other people. Pete and I connected once again and we soon developed a routine at Sunlea of watching footy together and enjoying the sunny garden. I remember Pete liked to listen to music, but at the time I didn't really like Richard Clayderman – Pete loved his music. We would all ask Pete to turn his music down or OFF.

When we both caught the school bus to head off to Talire and Douglas Parker School, Pete would be a bit agitated because he didn't like the bus. We had a black dog at Sunlea and Clive (the dog) would lick our hands and gulp down any leftover food.

Pete laughed when Clive licked his face.

Pete and I used to go for walks together with Clive on a lead and we would giggle when Clive wanted to run – which looked funny as he pulled one of our wheelchairs. We didn't talk to each other but once alone Pete and I knew how to communicate – words don't matter sometimes – especially for good mates like us.

During our time together at Sunlea, Pete and I loved to go to the beach and lie in our beanbags with our toes in the sand. Pete loved to sunbake.

When I left Sunlea to live in my own place Pete and I kept up our friendship. We played bowls at the bowling alley. We were very competitive especially when there was a trophy to take home.

One time, Pete came to stay overnight at my place. He slept on the couch. Mum had to come over a couple of times because Pete snored so loudly, he would trigger off the intercom!! I thought that was so funny – we didn't get much sleep that night.

I have so many memories of my good mate Pete – so many which can't be shared here today.

My friend Pete was a funny man. He liked jokes, he liked sport, he liked music, and he liked to lounge about in the garden.

My friend Pete will always be my mate; and I will miss him.

My friend Pete."

Chapter 52

Paul had various cancer treatments. He ate very little and had dramatic weight loss. His mood fluctuated, not surprisingly, then his spirits lifted again.

This cancer scare brought him to evaluate his life, past and future and he told Maxine that he was not afraid of dying. Paul had a dream of buying a little place in southern France and moving there to live.

'If you pay, I'll visit!' Maxine told him.

Paul had been in Maxine's life for forty years. She felt privileged spending time with him during his illness, sharing memories and deep conversations, giving her a strong sense of where they had been together in their lives. They both endured and enjoyed each other's company. Together they created innovative opportunities in the disability field, the Action Group, Sunlea and Don's program. Paul was also very helpful to Maxine in her early CEO days at Volunteering Tasmania.

Paul was always able to move from the small details to the big picture and back again, from one to the other. He was a first principles person; he considered the basic underlying principles and followed the logical thinking through.

Maxine was instinctive, practical and that made them a good

team over the years. Maxine could share her ideas with him and he would turn it into a document. She only had to say half a sentence and, yep, he got it. They were always like this. Paul had thought that, 'If you could bottle it, it would be good.'

Paul never found the sort of connection he had with Maxine, with anyone else. This was the case particularly with their intellectual meeting and their capacity to work together. As for their friendship, its solid basis was always there, profound. Also, just like moon cycles, over the years their friendship waxed and waned.

The last thing Maxine ever wanted was for her friends to offer a shoulder to cry on or offer her sympathy. Maxine wanted vigorous considered conversation and Paul gave her that. But after her husband died, Paul did turn up at her house with a bottle of scotch.

Paul became more social during his illness, a blessing for him and for those in his life. He went to the theatre and he and Maxine enjoyed a few evenings out together before he became too ill with treatment and surgery to do such things. He had a big gathering on the family farm, a living wake, with a bonfire and a spit roast and invited friends, family, and old colleagues to his farewell. He didn't want a funeral.

A few years earlier, Maxine had completed the enlivening Clinical Pastoral Care Course and volunteered with Hospice Tasmania, visiting and supporting individuals with terminal conditions. And here she was in the midst of family and friends' deaths.

Meanwhile her life and work went on and once more she had nine tonnes of beautiful wood delivered and stacked out the back, the annual squirrelling began.

By the end of September in 2017, Maxine turned sixty and she found it hard to watch Paul wasting away. His brother and sister were spending precious time with him and Maxine was grateful and deeply moved by his family and their respect for her and her friendship with Paul.

Maxine and Paul said their tender and honouring goodbyes. Paul slipped in and out of reality, it was difficult for him to speak or be understood, he was on strong pain medication, and struggled to swallow.

In the evening of 13 October 2017 Paul finally let go. Maxine was relieved and very sad; her mate was gone.

~

Then Tim, Maxine's brother, phoned her. She couldn't believe what she was being told. Just four days after Paul's death, and a few months after her mother's. It felt surreal.

Sherry, Maxine's sister hadn't been feeling well; she'd had a cold, was a bit breathless and made an appointment with her doctor on 17 October 2017. After the consultation she collapsed in the car park. The doctors and paramedics could not revive her. She was a young fifty-five-year-old.

Maxine helped organise, and then conduct, Sherry's funeral. She had given the eulogy at her husband's funeral at his request, and spoken at others. She was interested in conducting funerals but this was hard.

Three deaths in six months. What did it all mean or didn't it mean anything? Thankfully Don seemed okay.

~

There was the expected and the unexpected. Was death stalking her? Maxine was filled with apprehension again. *What might come next? Who might die next?* Thankfully Don seemed okay.

A year later, Maxine realised how much she missed Paul and his friendship, with its irritations and conversations, the innate understanding between them, the occasional dinners, the depth of meeting. She missed talking with him, especially now as she had to help with the transition of Don's program from the State-funded package of care to the NDIS: the negotiations both a repeat and an undoing of all that had come before.

It was patronising and frustrating to justify Don's needs again, when they had clearly been understood for so long. It felt like a step back to thirty years earlier. The process was emotionally damaging, and disrespectful of Don and Maxine.

Although the NDIS brought benefits for many with more choice and control over how people lived their lives, other families also experienced distress and trauma as they tried to negotiate support and services for their children. Some young people with disabilities were still stranded in residential aged-care facilities. The promised support and care were not provided.

The Royal Commission into Violence, Abuse, Neglect and Exploitation of People with Disability, was established in 2019. Many more appalling contemporary stories were told, nearly forty years after Maxine saved Don from the bleak Dickensian days of his life in the hospital institution.

Maxine knew that Don would only be better off if there was strong advocacy support. But she also knew that this could not be relied on. She was still scared for Don if she was no longer alive to once again make changes to his care.

Once NDIS support packages became available, new support providers were also established. Over time Maxine had come to understand that there was a clash of values with Beni Abbess and its management of Don's package. She had thought Beni Abbess was going to provide Don's ongoing lifelong support needs when she had walked back from the management of his program. But the organisation – being based on community principles – seemed more interested in the community of people in its care rather than any very specific individual needs.

So, once more Maxine had to find a new support provider more individually focused and sensitive to family involvement. The new provider was finally all that Maxine had hoped for, forming a wonderful team that loved Don and supported his day-to-day life. Maxine hoped this was truly the last change of Don's service provision and she could finally relax.

Chapter 53

Today, Maxine gardens. She digs; she makes vegetable patches with wheelbarrow loads of compost and chicken manure and straw mulch. She grows food and flowers and trees, propagates succulents and pots them. She plants out more bulbs in each new garden she creates as she moves home yet again, then waits and watches for green shoots in spring. She creates homes and fortresses for herself and when one gets breached, she creates another.

When anxious, Maxine walks the streets, fast paced, not afraid of the dark around the corner, across the causeway, by the river, softly rushing water by her side, stepping around occasional rocks along the sandy track under the trees. Despite her childhood horrors and neglect she always felt safe and looked after, outside in the dark.

She had no control over her own childhood. She had no power to say no; at one time she even stopped using her own words and surrendered into silence. When she met Don, it was almost a type of love affair taking place, a familiar heartbeat, dry mouth, damp eyes, and she gave her heart to him. His lack of words drove on her activism. Maxine asked politely, demanded, called out inconsistencies, contradictions, and never accepted no for an answer. No wasn't in her vocabulary She could not save her little brother's life but she saved Don's.

With her latest kitchen appliances handy and fresh herbs from her garden Maxine opens various cookbooks and plays with recipes. Creative flair in her cooking too. Today, her adolescent and young adult disordered eating, might have been diagnosed as an eating disorder. Her not eating was familiar, even a comfort. Would treatment have helped then or was her innate need for control a drive that helped her succeed in saving Don?

There have been crumblings in her adult years, the therapy years, the relationships with women and then Peter. Her marriage was another moment of taking control. For Maxine this normal act of commitment was radical, unexpected. Then that rock through her window triggered more anxiety.

~

Maxine is a thinker and a doer. She was born under the constellation of Leo, is a leader with a choleric temperament, drive and initiative, vision. If she can think it through, she will act on it. If it, whatever 'it' is can't be fixed, it is dropped. Gone. For Maxine actions are more important than words. A meal out, a trip away simply says thank you.

Feelings are buried deeper, not so visible, at times suppressed or even avoided by her enormous capacity for work. Her feeling life was crushed through childhood abuse; she retreated into herself, and out of her body.

She learnt to compartmentalise and contain parts of herself. During her therapy, Maxine discovered that emotion can undo us, strip us bare, and be exhausting. It can also bring relief, release and a breathing in after the letting go; it can build inner strength. Maxine hauled herself up out of generational trauma, her childhood and her grief. She developed the capacities to keep going, resilience.

She passionately grows things – plants and group homes, organisations, advocacy and independence for her son – and carries a burning fire for life. She creates change and comfortably swims with it, but if threatened, or if too much is expected of her, a rage can creep in and unsettle her. Her tone of voice still carries the sense of, 'No one tells me what to do,' but that has contracted, softened. Lately it is the occasional match head flare, then it burns down and is shaken out.

As Maxine travels into her late-sixties, while walking through the bush and on the beach, listening to music and writing, she reflects again. She recognises her over-responsibility as a child and adult, always looking out for, and skilfully interpreting other people's needs; those of her parents, siblings, friends and later, her lovers.

If she watched and waited and could not meet their needs, then it must have been her fault. Guilt reigned. *I am the forever adult looking after the forever child.* Her needs were repressed. But as an adult, occasionally her unrecognised needs rumble and spill out inappropriately, even making her ill. Her childhood survival strategies led to people pleasing. *I'm not doing that anymore.*

Maxine's strengths can also be flaws. Like many, she can sometimes be stubborn, immovable. And, it is also those qualities that, turned a different way, enabled her to pioneer so many changes in disability services. Occasionally there is a lack of insight, even a lack of empathy for others, and yet her empathy for the disadvantaged speaks volumes.

Fiercely independent, maybe strengthened by her solo

childhood wanderings in the bush and on the beaches, Maxine simply does her own thing.

Beside her ability to do what she needs for herself, she is exceptionally generous. At times she has separated herself from family, abandoned them, and yet is intensely loyal to her friends and her remaining family now. Like all of us, with incongruities, the capacities lie side-by-side.

She is known by many people and yes, has a few really close friends. Her life is lived in the public domain of Tasmania and she also guards her privacy intensely.

Maxine is a respected professional and is a survivor. There is both openness and a sense of being closed off at times. She is fearless and yet, she quavers. She is courageous and funny. And she has moments of prophetic dreams.

And Don? As he headed towards fifty his life was quieter but he was living a full life.

Maxine saved his life. By doing this, he also saved hers.

Epilogue

In June 2023 as Maxine talked with specialists about Don's care, she deeply missed Paul. Don's workers, and the coordinator of his program, were consulting with doctors and, finally, the palliative care team. Don had broken his hip. No one knew how it had happened, but he was diagnosed with weak bones, spasms, no muscle protection around his bones and a broken hip.

He had surgery, had a plate inserted, but there seemed to be ongoing pain, one lung collapsed then another, and he had pneumonia.

There were ongoing spasms and distress, maybe pain and rage, as he yelled, sounded out his experience. No words.

Pain medications were administered, his face softened, his body surrendered, he looked relaxed. No more agony, no more fighting for his rights, his care, his best possible life.

Maxine felt that as long as Don was comfortable, she could quietly creep into a place of acceptance.

On 24 June 2023, Don took a last breath. He looked peaceful. Finally, his frail body was at rest.

~

A gift emerged after Don's death. His two mothers tenderly reconnected. Maxine sent Don's birth mother photos of his life with her, and after his funeral and cremation, some of his ashes too. Both mothers were deeply grateful.

Don's birth mother gave him precious life and Maxine gave Don a meaningful flourishing life.

Acknowledgements

I am immensely grateful to friends and family who encourage my writing life.

Thank you, Maxine Griffiths, for your trust in me to share your story and for your endless patience.

Many Tasmanians shared their memories of Maxine and Don. I appreciate the considerable time and knowledge offered to me in interviews.

Warm thanks to Maxine's family including Maxwell Griffiths, Colleen Griffiths and Sherry McNamara (sadly all deceased) who gifted me their family stories.

Thank you to David Bowling, David Adams, Alison Jacob, Paul Kregor (deceased), and former Tasmanian Attorney General Judy Jackson for generous and insightful reflections.

Also, Rachel Greene for her history of Sunlea *Through The Window* and long-time Sunlea support worker Helen Haigh.

Sarah Armstrong and writers in her classes gave me their kind support and creative feedback as I explored a first draft of *Brick Walls*.

Thank you to terrific editors Laurel Cohn and Shelley Kenigsberg for their invaluable detailed expertise and guidance.

And Anna Featherstone for enthusiastic encouragement.

Sitting at writing desks looking out over gums and gardens and crafting words has been a joy and an adventure. I have been thrilled to be offered various mentorships and fellowships while writing *Brick Walls*. Thanks to the wonderful mentor Marele Day and my fellow writers awarded a Byron Writers Festival (formally the Northern Rivers Writers Centre) Residential Mentorship in 2015. They all gave caring encouragement, thoughtful feedback and we had fun writing days together.

I was selected for intensive programs for emerging writers including the MARION (formerly ACT Writers Centre) HARD-COPY Non-fiction program in 2015 and the QWC Publishable program in 2020. Thanks for their invaluable workshops, new colleagues and writing friends. And to Regional Arts NSW Quick Response Grant for financial support to attend HARDCOPY in Canberra.

I have also been awarded residential fellowships with Varuna, the glorious Writers' House in the Blue Mountains, and the Susannah Pritchard Centre in Perth. Thanks especially to the Varuna team for their warm-hearted hospitality and to the delightful creative company of other writers.

I am so fortunate to live and write on Bundjalung country in Northern NSW. The ocean breezes whisper to me of ancient lands and the original story tellers. I pay my respects to Elders both past and present.

www.ingramcontent.com/pod-product-compliance
Lightning Source LLC
LaVergne TN
LVHW041625060526
838200LV00040B/1435